TALL TALES FROM THE HIGH PLAINS & BEYOND
Book Three

The
LAWBREAKERS

TOM RIZZO
Author, *Last Stand At Bitter Creek*

TALL TALES FROM THE HIGH PLAINS & BEYOND
Book Three: The LawBreakers

ISBN-13: 978-0-9847977-6-9
ISBN-10: 0984797769

Cover Design & Interior Layout:
Studio 6 Sense, LLC • www.studio6sense.com

CONTENTS

INTRODUCTION

TALL TALES FROM THE HIGH PLAINS & BEYOND

Book One: The Unexplained and Other Stories

Book Two: The Law Keepers

Book Three: The LawBreakers

The public has a mostly a romanticized view of the *Old West,* or *Wild West,* as it was sometimes known. Western films and novels presented the American West as a place of gambling, gunfights, and Indian raids. Skillful writers and directors developed a formula of storytelling that resulted in perception overriding reality.

Most people who settled in the West didn't wake up in the morning and strap on a gun. Nor did they get involved in shootouts. There's no denying the West presented a rugged and untamed challenge. The characters, conflicts, and creations involved in the actual expansion and development of this new frontier represented fascinating raw material that played such an influential role in American history.

The three books that make up the series *Tall Tales from the High Plains & Beyond* offer short and entertaining stories aimed at giving you an Eagle's Nest view of the frontier and people who lived and died there. These men and women rival any character you'd meet in the pages of fiction.

- *Book One: The Unexplained and Other Stories* includes tales that border on the bizarre—ghosts, buried treasure, lost gold, a headless horseman, double- and triple-crosses, ambushes, mysterious disappearances, and stories of uncommon courage.

- *Book Two: The Law Keepers* features those who wore the badges of lawmen. Stories of courage, shootouts, showdowns, redemption, retribution, and sweet revenge. Lawmen who sometimes acted outside the law to achieve the desired results.

- *Book Three: The LawBreakers* who roamed the frontier as stone-cold killers, cattle and horse rustlers, bank, stagecoach, and train robbers. Some even tried stepping away from lives of crime and becoming lawmen. Most of those who did, however, discovered it put them in a better position as lawbreakers.

When I went to school, history was little more than memorizing names and facts and figures—an exercise in boredom. History isn't boring—particularly history of the American frontier. It falls to writers and teachers to bring these historical adventures to life, which is what I've tried to do with this series.

Enjoy!

ONE

A TARNISHED STAR

WHEN THE WESTBOUND ATCHISON, TOPEKA & SANTA FE EXPRESS ROLLED INTO A SMALL CATTLE STATION IN COOLIDGE, KANSAS, ON SEPTEMBER 29, 1883, SOMETIME AROUND 2 A.M., THREE MEN BOARDED, GUNS DRAWN.

The leader, holding a pistol in each hand, shoved one of them into John Hilton's chest and ordered him to stop the train. Hilton, a family man with a wife and four children hesitated a few seconds. The delay cost him his life. Without saying a word, the gunman pulled the trigger, sending a bullet into Hilton's heart. The bandit turned to the fireman, George Fadel, and shot him in the mouth or the neck with the other gun.

Well Fargo Express Manager Samuel Peterson spotted the gang approaching the express car and began shooting. The two sides exchanged about fifteen shots in a brief gun battle. Peterson sustained a slight wound but his aggressive action succeeded in driving the masked men away empty-handed.

Deputy Sheriff Dave Mather of Dodge City—also referred to as "Mysterious Dave"—assembled a posse and arrived in Coolidge to organize a search for the gunmen. Fadel, the train's fireman, managed to recover from his wound but wasn't much help in identifying the outlaws since they wore masks. Mather and his men eventually rounded up four suspects and put them behind bars in Dodge City.

Authorities tentatively identified the man they thought to be the one who killed the engineer as Lon Chambers. A former lawman, Chambers spent most of his career riding the Texas Panhandle as a cattle detective during the late 1870s. In 1881, he drifted into New Mexico where he joined Pat Garrett's posse to track down Billy the Kid and his gang. A couple of years after riding with Garrett, Chambers decided to take off the badge, form his own gang, and ride the outlaw trail.

No one knew the exact reason why Chambers switched sides. The decision most likely pivoted on crime being more lucrative than law enforcement. Little is known about the exploits of Chambers and his gang. The attempted train robbery at Coolidge stood as its most daring caper. Although Wells Fargo wouldn't confirm it, rumors indicated the express car safe carried $30,000. In Dodge City, Chambers and the others went on trial. But no one could provide hard evidence this particular group was responsible for the holdup. As a result, all four were released.

After that point, Lon Chambers vanished, his name never associated with another crime. He simply dropped out of sight—at least from the pages of history. Sadly, the cold-blooded outlaw who put an end to the life of engineer John Hilton got away with murder.

TWO

A THIRST
FOR VIOLENCE

W HEN HIS RANCH CAME INTO SIGHT NORTH OF PECOS, TEXAS,
CLAY ALLISON SLAPPED THE LEATHER REINS AGAINST THE
HORSES PULLING A FREIGHT WAGON IN HOPES HE COULD MAKE
UP FOR SOME LOST TIME.

As the speed increased, the load shifted and a grain sack fell
onto the roadway. Allison halted the team, jumped down, and
tried to retrieve the sack. He reached down but stumbled and fell
between the wheels of the wagon. The unexpected movement startled the horses and they bolted forward, dragging one of the wheels
across Allison's neck. Less than an hour later, on July 1, 1887, Clay
Allison died. His ignominious death—sudden and alone—was the
opposite of how he lived.

Born Robert A. Allison in 1840 in Waynesboro, Tennessee,
he spent the first couple of decades of his life farming. Allison's

father served as a Presbyterian minister, but he died when Clay was five. Allison joined the Confederacy in 1861 but got discharged because of a "mental condition." He later succeeded in rejoining a Confederate unit and worked as a scout.

When the war ended, he returned to his home and urged some family members to relocate to Texas with him. In Texas, Allison went to work for cattlemen *Oliver Loving and Charles Goodnight.* Then, he moved to Colfax County, New Mexico, in 1870 where he became a successful rancher. Allison's willingness for gunplay established him with a reputation as a professional shootist. Violence served as his constant companion. Although he got arrested several times, no charges ever stuck.

Allison was a short-tempered gunman given to violent mood swings. In October 1870, he led an angry mob of vigilantes who removed accused murderer Charles Kennedy from the local jail and hanged him. But Allison wasn't satisfied with just lynching the man. In a move the shocked the other vigilantes, he decapitated the dead man and displayed the man's head on a pole in a local saloon.

Four years later, in Santa Fe, Alison joined another lynch party that hanged suspected killer Cruz Vega. Seeing Vega dangling from the end of a rope didn't satisfy Allison, so he fired several shots into the dead man's back. The, he cut him down and dragged him over brush and rocks, mutilating it beyond recognition. A relative of Vega, Francisco "Pancho" Griego, considered a dangerous man, vowed revenge. The two men confronted each other at Lambert's Saloon in the St. James Hotel. Minutes later, Griego fell to the floor with three bullets in him.

The Cimarron *News and Press,* in January 1876, ran an editorial dressing down Allison. The piece so enraged Allison, he got drunk and stormed into the office and wrecked the place. Accounts say he later returned and paid $200 to cover the damages.

On December 21, 1876, with Christmas less than a week away, Clay Allison and his brother helped drive a herd into Las Animas, Colorado. Cold, tired, and thirsty, the Allison brothers headed for a saloon when Constable Charles Faber stopped them. "You'll have to give up those guns, gentlemen," said the Bent County officer. "City ordinance against carrying weapons."

The Allisons laughed, ignored the warning, and walked into the Olympic Dance Hall. Faber, in the meantime, deputized two bystanders and retrieved his shotgun. When the three walked into the dance hall, Faber leveled his shotgun and fired. John Allison fell to the floor from wounds to the chest and shoulder. His brother Clay whirled around, gun-in-hand, and snapped off four shots, killing Faber where he stood. The two newly appointed deputies fled.

James Reasoner, in his book *Draw: The Greatest Gunfights of the American West,* wrote that Allison "grabbed the dead deputy by the hair" and dragged him over to his wounded brother. "John, this is the son of a bitch who shot you," Clay said. "I got him, all right. Everything's going to be all right. Don't you fret." His brother eventually recovered.

When Sheriff John Spiers heard about the shooting, he arrested the Allison brothers and jailed them. A coroner's jury charged them with murder, even though John Allison hadn't fired a shot. The charge, however, was later dropped. Prosecutors changed the charge against Clay Allison from murder to manslaughter. Witnesses pointed out that Faber fired into the crowd at the Olympic without warning. Allison and his brother, who recovered from the wound, were taken into custody.

By March 1877, no one had come forward to testify against Allison and prosecutors released him on a $10,000 bond. According to Frank Clifford in his book *Deep Trails in the Old West: A Frontier Memoir,* Clay Allison never used a gun in anger after the Las Animas shootout.

Most men seem to mellow with age. Allison proved the exception. The older he got, the meaner he became. Allison once rode into Cheyenne, Wyoming, with a toothache causing him unbearable pain. On the way in, he chose the nearest of the town's two dentists. When the dentist accidentally drilled into the wrong molar, the patient got angry, leaped out of the chair, and left to see Cheyenne's other dentist. After the problem was resolved, Allison returned to the first dentist's office, shoved him into his own chair, grabbed a forceps, and tried pulling out the dentist's teeth. Depending on the version of the story you read, the dentist's screams apparently alerted the townspeople who rescued him.

In the summer of 1878, Allison and lawman Wyatt Earp supposedly confronted each other. Different versions of the so-called showdown exist, including an account by the San Francisco *Examiner*, in an interview with Earp that appeared August 16, 1896. Details of the face-off are included in various biographies of Earp. Pinkerton agent Charles Siringo included one in his autobiography. In his version, Allison seems to get the upper hand on Earp. The *Ford County Historical Society* of Dodge City, Kansas, published the account as, *The True Story of Clay Allison and Wyatt Earp Dodge City, KS.*

THREE

ROWDY JOE & RED BEARD

OWDY JOE LOWE STOOD AT THE BAR OF THE WICHITA, KANSAS, DANCE HALL HE OWNED WHEN A GUNSHOT SHATTERED THE EAST WINDOW, THE BULLET SLICING ACROSS THE LOWER PART OF HIS NECK.

Bleeding and angry, he snatched up his shotgun and headed for the saloon next door. He charged into the competing dance hall and demanded to know who shot him.

"I done it," admitted a liquored-up saloon owner Edward "Red" Beard, waving his six-gun.

Without a word, Lowe fired off both barrels over the heads of those crowded inside, scattering dance hall girls and cowboys. Just as Beard raised his revolver to return fire, Rowdy Joe's wife, Kate, barged in and dragged her husband outside. Although witnesses testified Lowe had only been trying to scare Beard, some of the buckshot hit patron Billie Anderson in the head, permanently blinding him.

Lowe was the first of the two to open a saloon and bawdyhouse. Beard followed a short time later and the rival dance halls found themselves competing for the same clientele. The rivalry changed, however, when angry Union soldiers destroyed Beard's saloon by burning it to the ground. By the time he rebuilt, Lowe's operation was going strong, raking in most of the available dollars.

The two men feuded. Tempers flared. Threats were leveled, and, bad blood boiled. Both had reputations as gunmen and had killed others in various disputes. On the night of October 27, 1873, Red Beard's frustration grew to the point when, in a drunken stupor, he glanced out the door and saw Lowe standing at the bar of his place. That's when he squeezed off the shot that grazed Lowe's neck.

Accounts differ on specifics, but most generally agree that, after the shooting, Beard turned his wrath on dance hall girl Josephine "Miss Jo" DeMerritt, his one-time mistress, accusing her of either working against him or stealing from him. Whatever the case, Beard reportedly began roughing her up before a couple of customers came to her rescue. But that didn't quell Beard's infamous temper. According to one story, when Miss Jo fled either to the back of his place or to Lowe's next door, Beard took at shot at her. The bullet missed but struck another dance hall girl, Annie Franklin, in the stomach.

Beard and Lowe eventually confronted each other as the clock moved past midnight. Beard was later discovered bleeding heavily from wounds to the hip and arm. He died two weeks later. Lowe was cleared of the shooting and, along with his wife Kate, left town. The couple ended up in Dodge City, Tombstone, and eventually to Denver, Colorado, where a policeman killed him in 1899.

FOUR

WANTED: COAL OIL JIMMY

NO ONE SEEMED TO KNOW HOW *COAL OIL JIMMY* GOT HIS NICK-NAME, BUT IT HAD NOTHING TO DO WITH HIS OCCUPATION OR REPUTATION.

James Buckner, his real name, and an associate by the name of Frank Taylor, also known as *Barber*, made their living by robbing, rustling cattle, and committing murder in northern New Mexico. The two men staged a series of stagecoach robberies on the road to Cimarron. Around October 17, 1871, they forced the Santa Fe mail coach to a stop near Vermejo Stage Station in Colfax County and robbed it and the passengers.

The territorial governor wasted no time in distributing a wanted poster offering a $600 reward for the capture of Coal Oil Jimmy. The Maxwell Land Grant Company and the Barlow & Sanderson Stage Line upped the ante. Altogether, authorities posted a $3,000 award, dead or alive. According to various newspapers, Buckner and Taylor generally made life difficult, roughed people up, turned violent on some occasions, and "threatened the lives of several of our citizens" throughout the area.

Although Buckner made his home in Elizabethtown, he and Taylor decided to head for Ute Park after the robbery and lay low for a while. In late November, Jim McIntyre and Frank Stewart rode into Ute Park, made contact with Buckner and Taylor, and floated the idea of forming a gang. The two robbers liked the idea and suggested they all meet in the Turkey Mountains, east of Fort Union, to talk it over and a develop a plan to steal horses as the new gang's first venture.

In reality, McIntyre and Stewart were Texas bounty hunters seeking to cash in on the reward. While Coal Oil Jimmy was sleeping, his accomplice Taylor stood near the fire trying to keep warm. The two bounty hunters took advantage of the situation. With the outlaws' guard down, the two men drew their guns, and fired away, killing both Buckner and Taylor with bullets to the head.

In an editorial following the shooting, the *Santa Fe Weekly New Mexican* wrote that it hoped other "evil parties" throughout the community "will take warning from the fate of these two men and seek some honest mode of making a livelihood."

FIVE

DARING
BRACK CORNETT

O N A COLD WEDNESDAY MORNING, FEBRUARY 15, 1888, A MAN
WALKED INTO THE BANK OF CISCO, TEXAS, JUST BEFORE CLOS-
ING TIME ASKING FOR CHANGE. BEFORE CASHIER C.C. LEVEAUX
COULD FULFILL THE REQUEST, HE LOOKED UP AND SAW THREE MORE
MEN HURRY THROUGH THE DOOR, GUNS DRAWN.

The Bill Whitley Gang—sometimes called the Brack Cornett
Gang—walked out the door with around $9,000 in gold, silver, and
bank notes and escaped to the northwest. Formed about a year
before the Cisco heist, the 12-member gang pulled off a series of
bank and train robberies that netted thousands upon thousands
of dollars. A few days after the Cisco holdup, the gang traveled
about two-hundred miles downstate where they boarded the I&GN
train near McNeill in Travis County and took $20,000 from the
express car.

The gang laid low until June when Brack Cornett, calling himself *Captain Dick*, robbed the Southern Pacific near Schulenburg, Texas, described by the *New York Times* as "the most daring train robbery that ever occurred in Texas." Cornett was considered the most well-known member of Whitley's gang. Rather than lay low for a while, success only fed the greed and the gang decided to stage a raid on the Southern Pacific train at Harwood, about sixty miles east of San Antonio.

US Marshal John Rankin, however, got wind of the plan. Rankin, Deputy Duval West, and several Texas Rangers, boarded the train on September 22nd and surprised the gang when it stopped the train three miles outside Harwood. Gang members fled. A day or two later, however, the gang robbed a train near Flatonia.

On September 25th, a contingent of US Marshals caught up to the gang at Floresville in Wilson County, and exchanged gunfire. Whitley was killed. One of the gang was taken into custody, but Cornett escaped alone on horseback and headed into Arizona Territory. The task of tracking down Cornett fell to lawmen Alfred Allee. A former Texas Ranger, Allee worked as a lawman in Karnes and Frio counties in Texas.

Allee had the reputation of being bad-tempered and suspected of shooting those he arrested even after surrendering. He was also known as a racist. Once, when boarding a train, a black porter bumped into him and Allee shot and killed him. He was arrested, tried, but acquitted. When Allee caught up with Cornett, the two shot it out on horseback and Cornett died. Allee, in 1896, was killed after being stabbed in a barroom brawl in Laredo, Texas.

SIX

A RAGE
IN CATOOSA

NO ONE KNEW WHAT TOUCHED OFF THE FISTFIGHT BETWEEN THE TWO MEN AT A POOL HALL IN CATOOSA, OKLAHOMA, BUT IT MARKED THE BEGINNING OF A NIGHT OF TERROR IN THE INDIAN TERRITORY COMMUNITY.

Deputy Constable Jess W. Elliot of the Cherokee Nation police rode into Catoosa on November 3, 1892, to serve legal papers. Elliot, who also practiced law, dropped by the pool hall, had too much to drink, and got into an argument with a ranch hand named Bob Rogers. Fists flew and Rogers quickly got the upper hand. He floored Elliot and continued beating him before several men pulled him away and escorted him outside to his horse.

After Elliott regained consciousness, he managed to sober up enough to leave and head home to Vinita, where the 40-year old part-Cherokee lawman lived. Rogers, in the meantime, waited in ambush to attack Elliot. After forcing the constable from his horse, Rogers leaped down off his own mount, drew his knife, and slashed Elliot across his throat three times and left him to die in the middle of the roadway. A traveler, who saw Rogers ride away, found Elliot but couldn't help. The man had lost too much blood. The stranger alerted authorities in Catoosa who sent for Deputy US Marshal John Taylor. A local doctor and several others rode out to the scene of the crime, built a fire, and decided to stay with the body until Taylor's arrival.

A short while later, the group heard hoof beats approaching and watched with fear and surprise as Bob Rogers spurred his horse through the flames, scattering the group. Rogers leaped off his horse, and attacked Elliot's corpse. In a display of rage, he stomped the body, ripped the legal documents Elliot carried from the man's pockets, snatched the hat from the dead man's head, and fled. Taylor trailed Rogers for a while but lost him.

Rogers' life of crime began in his teens when he stole about a dozen horses in Indian Territory, drove them into Arkansas, and sold them. But the law caught up with him and took him to Fort Smith to face federal judge Isaac Parker. Since Rogers was only 19 and this was his first offense, the judge gave him a break and suspended his prison sentence. He placed Rogers on probation and delivered a stern lecture, warning him that if he continued breaking the law, "...death may be the penalty." Rogers ignored the advice and, in the fall of 1891, was charged with assault for attempting to kill a lawman. But, again he got a break, and was released on bond.

After killing lawman Elliot, the psychopathic Rogers formed a gang that included his two brothers and swept across Kansas and Oklahoma Territory stealing horses, rustling cattle, and robbing banks, and merchants. On March 13, 1895, a large posse tracked Rogers to his father's home where he had been hiding. When two deputies entered the house to take him into custody, he opened fire and shot two of them.

A shootout followed. Historians say the posse riddled the home with between two-hundred and three-hundred rounds. The firepower was so furious, it cut some of the rafters into two. A while later, Rogers agreed to give up. He walked out of the house carrying his Winchester. When he lifted the rifle, the entire posse began firing and he went down with twenty-two bullets and two shotgun blasts.

SEVEN

THE OUTLAW WHO
TALKED WITH CHRIST

O UTLAW AND LAWMAN JAMES MCINTIRE CLAIMED HE ONCE DIED, WENT TO HEAVEN AND ENGAGED IN A FACE-TO-FACE CHAT WITH CHRIST WHO THEN ALLOWED HIM TO RETURN TO HIS BODY FOR SEVERAL MORE YEARS.

McIntire outlined his near-death experience in a 1902 autobiography, *Early Days in Texas: A Trip Through Hell and Heaven*. He decided to write the book after surviving a smallpox epidemic that struck the Oklahoma community where he lived in 1901. The story never caught on with the public and didn't sell many copies probably because of McIntire's reputation for a vivid imagination. For example, McIntire told about the time he served as deputy sheriff of Mobeetie, Texas, and ran two deadly gunmen out of town for trying to run a scam selling phony gold bricks. He identified the two scammers as Wyatt Earp and Mysterious Dave Mather.

McIntire's revelations include a few shocking anecdotes, such as seeing a companion killed and eaten by Comanche warriors and about the time he fashioned a purse from the breast of a Comanche woman. Although these stories raised questions about his credibility, McIntire wore many hats on his Western adventure and straddled both sides of law and order. Pinkerton Detective Charles Siringo, in his own book, described McIntire as a man with "a nervous disposition" who "had shot and killed several men." Others described him as quick-on-the-trigger.

Born in Brown County, Ohio, in 1854, McIntire's real name was Isaac but he preferred his father's name, *Jim* or *James*. As a teenager, he tried his hand as a telegraph operator and later worked on steamboats on the Ohio River. Seeking more adventure, McIntire headed west in 1873. He spent time ranching and hunting buffalo and got involved into the sheep-herding business. Eventually, he settled in Mobeetie for a while to run a saloon. He also won election to the Wheeler County Commission.

In 1879, McIntire traveled to Dodge City, Kansas, to join Ford County Sheriff Bat Masterson who organized a group of gunmen on behalf of the Atchison, Topeka & Santa Fe Railroad in a battle over access rights to silver mines in Leadville, Colorado. During McIntire's colorful career, he served as a Texas Rangers, became city marshal of Las Vegas, New Mexico, fought Indians, and turned outlaw. Authorities once posted a one-thousand dollar reward for his capture due to his involvement in the deaths of two men near Silver City, New Mexico.

According to McIntire, his adventures included run-ins or associations with gunfighters Bill the Kid, "Longhair Jim" Courtright, Sam Bass, "Mysterious Dave" Mather, and Dave Rudabaugh. He eventually married and settled in Mountain View, Oklahoma. After his book was published, McIntire dropped out of sight. It's believed he died between 1910 and 1916, but exactly how and where he died is unknown.

EIGHT

THE CAPER
AT CASTLE GATE

A FEW PEOPLE NOTICED, BUT NO ONE QUESTIONED THE PECULIAR CONDUCT OF A COUPLE OF STRANGERS WHO HAPPENED TO VISIT THE CASTLE GATE, UTAH, TRAIN DEPOT EVERY AFTERNOON FOR A WEEK TO WATCH THE ARRIVAL OF THE DENVER & RIO GRANDE WESTERN FROM SALT LAKE CITY.

Castle Gate, a large coal-mining town in Carbon County in eastern Utah, was named for the rock formation near the narrow opening to Price Canyon. Two sheer sandstone walls flanked the Price River, giving the appearance of a giant gate. Officials of the Pleasant Valley Coal Company, which owned the mine, always felt a little edgy on paydays because Castle Gate stood between two well-know outlaw hideouts—Brown's Hole and Robber's Roost. Miners, in fact, never knew what days they'd be paid. Company officials routinely changed the payday to discourage robbery attempts.

Even paymaster E.L. Carpenter didn't always know when the payroll train would arrive from Salt Lake City. Precautions were also in place for the trains to be well guarded.

At a mid-morning in the second week of April 1897, Butch Cassidy and Elza (or *Elzy*) Lay rode into town, stopped at the saloon for a while, and then rode their unsaddled horses down to the train station. They repeated the routine every day for nearly a week. Cassidy, leader of the Wild Bunch, rarely attempted a robbery without a well-thought-out plan. He didn't like loose ends. His preparation involved not only the robbery itself but an escape strategy as well. He knew it would be pointless to attempt to rob the train along the way because he wouldn't know which train transported the payroll. His wait-and-see strategy paid off.

When the DRGW pulled into Castle Gate on a clear, sunny Wednesday, April 21st, Cassidy heard a whistle blast—the signal to miners they would be paid later in the day. Paymaster Carpenter and an assistant gathered the payroll bags containing about $7,000 in twenty-dollar gold pieces, currency, and silver, and walked toward the company office, located on the second floor of a stone building seventy-five yards away. Butch Cassidy fell in behind them and shoved his Colt .45 into Carpenter's rib, with a quiet warning.

"I'll take the money bags, sir. Stay calm since I'd have to shoot a hole in you."

Elza Lay sat on his horse a few feet away and watched as Carpenter let the bags of gold fall to the ground. The assistant dropped the bag of silver he was holding. When Cassidy walked over to hand some of the loot to Lay, the paymaster ran up the stairs toward the office yelling a warning about the robbery. A shot was fired. Cassidy's horse spooked. But he and Lay managed to make their way out through the steep and narrow canyon with the payroll. They left behind the bag of silver because it was too heavy to lug along. Mining company officials tried to telegraph the county sheriff but other members of Cassidy's gang cut the lines.

The Castle Gate caper proved the first of eight major robberies committed by the Wild Bunch between 1897 and 1901. At that point, Cassidy and one of his partners, Harry Alonzo Longabaugh, also known as the Sundance Kid, saw the writing on the wall. Authorities, thanks to more sophisticated communication, began improving their tracking skills, closing in on the gang.

To avoid frontier lawmen, Cassidy and Longabaugh left for South America in February 1901. Once they were gone, most of the remaining members of the Wild Bunch either went to jail or were killed.

NINE

HANGING AT HELL GATE

CYRUS SKINNER SPENT MOST OF HIS LIFE REIGNING TERROR ON OTHERS UNTIL A COLD WINTER NIGHT IN 1864 WHEN LADY JUSTICE RODE INTO A PLACE CALLED HELL GATE, MONTANA, LOOKING FOR HIM.

Skinner, born in Ohio in 1829, began his career in crime as a teen-ager robbing people. When he was 21, he moved to California where he got arrested for burglary and sentenced to the state prison at San Quentin. Two years later, on August 18, 1853, he was released. After six months of freedom, Skinner took up where he left off. And, as before, he found himself behind bars at San Quention once again for committing burglary. He wouldn't serve the full three-year sentence, however, because he escaped and committed another five robberies. Once again, authorities caught up to him. This time, the court slapped him with a fifteen-year jail term at San Quentin. But, as before, he managed to escape.

In the spring of 1860, Skinner headed for the gold camps of Idaho where he joined outlaw Henry Plummer who headed a gang that plundered miners and travelers. It wasn't long before Skinner began feeling the heat from Idaho authorities and left for the gold fields of Montana where he opened saloons at Bannack and Virginia City. Plummer and his road agents soon followed Skinner into Montana. Together, they began a reign of terror, robbing and killing Montanans. Skinner was considered among the most brutal of the Plummer gang, reportedly murdering others "just for the fun of it." Some reports contend the gang killed at least a hundred people.

Thomas Dimsdale, editor of the *Montana Post* in Virginia City, described Skinner as a "blood-thirsty and malignant outlaw, without a redeeming quality... a hardened, merciless and brutal fiend." During the crime wave, Plummer kept a low profile and, ironically, became the sheriff of Bannack.

Skinner used the profits from his businesses, and no doubt from the crimes he committed, to invest in mining claims and supposedly did quite well. But the citizens of Bannack and Virginia City had enough and decided to strike back at the unrelenting crime wave. A group of them secretly organized the Montana Vigilantes and proceeded to dispense their own brand of law and order—vigilante justice. Wearing masks and striking in the middle of the night, the vigilantes went calling on suspected outlaws. At first, they issued warnings. Then, they began to lynch suspects they found guilty. They caught up with Plummer on January 10, 1864, and hanged him and two partners.

Skinner, fearful of being caught up in this brand of swift justice, sold his businesses and moved to Hell Gate where he reopened a saloon that had been shuttered the year before. But the vigilantes weren't far behind. They tracked down Skinner later that same month, held a three-hour mock trial, and judged him guilty. Despite the verdict, he denied the accusations. Sometime after midnight, they hustled Skinner and two associates to a make-shift gallows at Higgins corral. While making their way to the cor-ral, Skinner suddenly broke free from one of his guards and took off running.

Not able to stand the thought of dying by a hangman's noose, he shouted, "Shoot! Shoot!," hoping the vigilantes would gun him down. But his captors caught up to him. Skinner and the other two, Alex Carter and Johnny Cooper, were among the last of the twenty-four suspected outlaws the vigilantes hanged.

TEN

THE WHITE CAPS GANG

A COLD WIND SWEPT THROUGH THE DESERTED STREETS OF LASVEGAS, NEW MEXICO, ON THE NIGHT OF OCTOBER 22,1892, AS THREE GUNMEN DRAGGED ONE OF THEIR OWN GANG MEMBERS THROUGH THE SNOW TO THE TOWN BRIDGE WHERE THEY HANGED HIM.

The next day, the citizens of Las Vegas awakened to see their streets bathed in brilliant sunshine and coated by a layer of snow and ice. They also spotted the frozen body of Patricio Maes swinging by his neck from a metal beam of the Gallinas River Bridge. Maes belonged to a gang known as the White Caps, also known as Forty Bandits, or Society of Bandits. During the late 1880s and early 1890s, this mob of outlaws waged terror throughout the region trying to drive settlers from lands once considered common pasture. In addition to physical intimidation, the gang cut fences, set fires to homes and outbuildings, and carried out other organized-crime type of activities.

The leader of the White Caps, unknown to anyone but gang members, ran a successful business in town. Silva Vincente, respected and well-liked, operated the Imperial Saloon. Handsome, large-framed, and red-bearded, no one suspected this family man as the underworld godfather behind a series of cattle rustling and unsolved murders. Vincente called a meeting of the White Caps on the night of the hanging and staged what amounted to a kangaroo court on the second floor of his saloon where Maes stood accused of being an informer.

When Vincente handed down the verdict, he ordered Jose Chavez y Chavez, Eugenio Alarid, and Julian Trujillo to carry out the execution. All three were members of the local police department. Several months later, Vincente suspected his brother-in-law, Gabriel Sandoval, might be on the verge of revealing what he knew about the White Caps and the Maes hanging. Sandoval worked as a bartender at the Imperial. Vincente decided to take no chances on whether his suspicions were true. He again summoned the three crooked lawmen to handle the problem. In February 1893, Sandoval was shot and killed and his body disappeared. Vincente's wife, Telesfora, distraught over her missing brother, began asking questions—too many. Her curiosity put her on death's doorstep.

Vincente, who had been in hiding because of several accusations leveled against him, sent for his wife. When she arrived, her husband demanded all the money she carried, which amounted to about two-hundred dollars. And, then he stabbed her to death. Vincente, as before, called on the three outlaw-lawmen and ordered them to dig a grave for her. Disgruntled over the meager ten-dollars their boss paid them, the three of them killed him and buried his body along with his wife's.

With the White Caps leaderless, the gang disbanded. Eventually, Chavez, Alarid, and Trujillo were arrested and charged with the murder of Maes. All three were sent to prison to serve life sentences.

ELEVEN

MAN IN THE MUSLIN MASK

THE CALIFORNIA-BOUND STAGECOACH LEFT PRESCOTT, ARIZONA, JUST AFTER DAWN ON SEPTEMBER 27, 1877, AND TRAVELED UNTIL LATE AFTERNOON WHEN A LONE HIGHWAYMAN ARMED WITH A SHOTGUN AND REVOLVER STEPPED OUT OF THE SHADOWS AND ORDERED THE DRIVER TO STOP.

The gunman, face and head wrapped with black gauze to hide his features, ordered two of the passengers to throw out the express box and the mailbags. He handed an axe to one passenger and told him to break the express box open. Another passenger was ordered to slit open the mailbags.

Although it was rare for any road agent to hold-up a stagecoach single-handedly, William "Brazen Bill" Brazelton managed to do it several times. On this, his first attempt, he came away with around $2,500 in gold dust, gold bars, and cash he took from the mail.

He moved on to New Mexico to stage similar hold-ups, but then returned to Arizona to use the Tucson area as a base of operations. Brazelton traded the black gauze for a more durable mask that had eyeholes cut out and a red mouth sewn on. He also made the acquaintance of a young rancher by the name of David Nemitz who felt pressured to become accessory to the robberies. Brazleton needed Nemitz' place so he stable his horse and stock supplies.

In August of the following year, Brazen Bill struck a stagecoach northwest of Tucson that carried John P. Clum, owner and editor of the Tombstone Epitaph. Clum later wrote: "....never until day before yesterday have we had the good fortune to witness the modus operandi by which these members of the shotgun gentry extract the valuables from a stage coach and passengers by the simple magical persuasive power of cold lead."

Authorities discovered the tracks of two horses at the scene of the robbery, but no tracks from that point on. An expert tracker learned the horse threw a shoe leaving impressions in the road of an animal "with three shod hoofs traveling in one direction and the fourth unshod hood in the opposite direction." Tracker Juan Elias determined that Brazelton apparently made the shoes for this particular purpose. Four nail holes on each side of each shoe were spaced so accurately that when the shoes were reversed, nails could be pushed through the same holes in the horse's hoof. Elias tracked the horse to Nemitz' corral. The sheriff arrested him as an accessory.

Nemitz agreed to help bring Brazelton into custody if he could be assured protection from the man he feared would kill him. Nemitz revealed that he and Brazelton were supposed to meet later. Nemitz also warned the sheriff that Brazelton should not be taken alive.

Pima County Sheriff Charles A. Shibell and a six-man posse moved out under cover of darkness that night to the rendezvous point where Nemitz was supposed to meet Brazelton with supplies.

Brazelton arrived packing a Spencer rifle, a couple of six-shooters, and two belts filled with cartridges. He coughed a couple of times—a signal to Nemitz. But something alarmed him and he spotted one of the posse members. Before he could act, a shotgun roared and flashed in the darkness. Brazelton fell from his horse.

"I die bravely, my God! I'll pray till I die," he muttered.

The posse waited in the dark, fearing some kind of retaliation. But, Brazen Bill was dead. Later on, his body—riddled with ten holes between his shoulders and heart—was taken to Tucson, strapped to a chair, and displayed at the courthouse until an inquest could be held.

TWELVE

LETTERS FROM BILLY THE KID

"DEAR SIR, I WOULD LIKE TO SEE YOU FOR A FEW MOMENTS IF YOU CAN SPARE THE TIME. YOURS RESPECT-W.H. BONNEY."

Adjusting his glasses, New Mexico Territory Governor Lew Wallace put the March 2, 1881, letter aside and picked up another letter from Bonney, this one dated two days after the first. "...I Expect you have forgotten what you promised me, this Month two years ago, but I have not and I think you had ought to have come and seen me as I requested you to." Bonney, better known as *Billy the Kid*, expressed disappointment in the letter that although he fulfilled every promise he made to Wallace, he had the feeling the governor left him out in the cold.

Wallace, a Civil War veteran and popular author, took the job of governor of New Mexico Territory in 1878, replacing Samuel Axtell, who had been accused of corruption. Wallace's first priority:

diffuse the Lincoln County Wars, a conflict centered on economic control of the area that turned violent and deadly. The governor wasted no time in pressing for a solution. He offered rewards, signed death warrants, and organized civilian militias in an effort resolve the turmoil.

Each side hired gunfighters to strengthen their firepower, William Bonney among them. The conflict eased for a while, but the murder of attorney Huston Chapman in February 1879 triggered renewed violence. Assuming the role of lead investigator in the killing, Governor Wallace personally interviewed those involved. Bonney, who had witnessed Chapman's murder, tried to make a deal with Wallace for amnesty in exchange for his testimony. Wallace accepted, but only if Bonney agreed to stand trial for crimes for which he had already been indicted. The situation, however, began to unravel when Bonney's testimony proved worthless.

Worried that Wallace wouldn't hold up his end of the deal, Billy the Kid decided the best option was escape. He was eventually captured in December 1880, and brought to trial. Cooling his heels in the Santa Fe Jail, Bonney wrote four letters to Wallace trying to renew his original agreement. But the governor opted not to reply. Convicted of murdering Lincoln County Sheriff William Brady, Bonney was sentenced to hang. Wallace personally drafted the death warrant. But nothing came of it because Bonney escaped, killing two jail guards in the process. The same year, Sheriff Pat Garrett tracked him down and killed him.

Wallace, the 11th governor of the New Mexico Territory, proved accomplished in several different careers. In addition to demonstrating his savvy as a politician, he built a reputation as a distinguished author. In 1873, Wallace wrote his first novel, *The Fair God*, a romantic tale of the Spanish conquest of Mexico. During his years as governor, Wallace finished his most famous novel, *Ben Hur: A Tale of the Christ* (1880). The novel became one of the most popular and best selling in history. He also wrote *The Prince of India* (1893), dealing with the Wandering Jew, (a character in Christian legend) and the Byzantine Empire. He completed several more books during his two years at the Palace of the Governors.

President James Garfield, who had read *Ben Hur,* appointed Wallace to serve as U.S. Minister Resident to the Ottoman Empire. Garfield said he couldn't think of a more qualified person for the position based on the author's familiarity with the customs, and geography, of the eastern Mediterranean.

THIRTEEN

BIG, BALD, AND BOASTFUL

THE BIG MAN SLID HIS GUN FROM THE RIGHT HOLSTER, AIMED AT THE BEER BOTTLE SWAYING FROM THE TREE LIMB, AND SQUEEZED THE TRIGGER. THE STRING SNAPPED. AS THE BOTTLE DROPPED, HE YANKED THE OTHER SIX-GUN WITH HIS LEFT HAND AND FIRED, SHATTERING THE BOTTLE BEFORE IT HIT THE GROUND.

The crowd roared with approval, which delighted Burt Alvord who spent most of his life as a lawman, train robber, and fugitive. The son of a justice of the peace, Burt Alvord was born in Arizona Territory in 1866 and grew up around Casa Grande. At 15, Alvord got a job as a stable hand at the OK Corral in Tombstone and witnessed the famous gunfight. Three years later, he watched vigilantes string up John Heath, a convicted thief and murderer.

Blessed with a big ego, the square-shouldered and bald Alvord worked as a lawman in his youth. When city officials in the mining community of Pearce heard about his skills with guns and fists, they hired him as constable. It didn't take him long to push his weight around and bring law and order to the mining crowd. His reputation caught the attention of the folks in Willcox and in Fairbank where he was hired to achieve the same results. And he did. His skills as a tracker helped Alvord round up, or kill, several cattle rustlers and outlaws between 1886 and 1889.

Alvord couldn't handle success. He began drinking heavily, to the point of alcoholism. With demon rum clouding judgment, Alvord decided he could make a better living robbing trains. But, he would keep his job as a law officer and no one would be the wiser. Before long, he put together a gang consisting of Billy Stiles, "Three-Fingered Jack" Dunlop, Bill Downing, Matt Burts, and Bravo Juan Yoas.

The gang's first score took place on the night of September 11, 1899, when they robbed a train at Cochise Station and got away with as much as $30,000 in gold. When the robbery occurred, Alvord, Stiles, Burts, and Downing were supposedly playing poker in a back room at Schwertner's Saloon. In mid-game, they crawled out a side window, held up the Union Pacific, and returned to sneak back in and resume playing. A few folks rushed into the saloon to tell Constable Alvord about the holdup. Displaying shock, Alvord quickly formed a posse, deputizing his poker-playing partners. Feeling flush with success at his first attempt robbing a train, Alvord decided to do it again, and targeted the train station at Fairbank on the evening of February 15, 1900.

Jeff Milton, a former lawman who went to work for the railroad as an express messenger, thwarted the robbery. Dunlop was killed and Yoas wounded. Alvord and the others were rounded up and put behind bars in Tombstone. Historians say Stiles agreed to testify against the others, but ended up helping Alvord and a couple dozen other prisoners escape. Alvord and Stiles eventually surrendered in late 1902. In exchange for a reduced sentence and the reward money, Alvord struck a deal to help the Arizona Rangers capture Mexican bandit Augustine Chacon. After his capture, however, the pair returned to their outlaw ways.

They were captured in 1903 but, once again, escaped. The Rangers pursued them into Mexico and re-captured them. Alvord spent the next couple of years in prison. After his release, he fled to South America, reportedly where he died. In 1907, a cattle rustler killed a Nevada deputy sheriff by the name of William Larkin. The deputy's widow revealed that William Larkin was actually Billy Stiles.

FOURTEEN

MASSACRE AT DEVIL'S KITCHEN

EYEING A BIG PAY-DAY, THE JIM HUGHES GANG WAITED IN AMBUSH AT DEVIL'S KITCHEN, SITUATED AT THE WEST END OF WHAT WOULD LATER BE CALLED SKELETON CANYON.

Below, a group of Mexican bandits known as the Estrada Gang made camp to enjoy a siesta in the hot afternoon sun of July 1881. The canyon, in the far southeast corner of Arizona, served as a corridor to smuggle goods into the U.S. to sell on the black market. Hughes, a week or so before, overheard members of the Estrada Gang making plans to smuggle a sizable amount of loot into the U.S. Wasting no time, he recruited his own gang to spring an ambush and take the treasure.

When the Mexicans dozed off, Hughes' men began shooting in what turned out to be one of the worst massacres in Arizona history. After the echo of gunfire faded, nineteen Mexicans lay dead on the canyon floor. When the mules carrying the loot bolted during the gunfire, gang members shot them down as well to keep them from scattering. Twenty-six mules were killed. Killing the mules, however, created a problem. Since they were all dead, the Hughes Gang had no way to transport the gold coins, jewelry, and various artifacts, which was believed to amount to around $75,000.

They divvied up what they could carry, buried the rest of the riches, and decided to return later. Hughes, however, made other plans. He got together with Zwing Hunt and Billy Grounds to pull a double-cross. While Hughes stayed in Galeyville, Arizona, to keep the rest of the gang from getting suspicious, his two allies would return to the site, dig up the loot, and rebury it somewhere only the three of them know about. Zwing and Hunt, fearing retaliation from the other gang members, decided on a double-double cross. They dug up the money and reburied it in a spot only they knew. The pair then fled to a desert cave to hide out for several months until it was safe to retrieve the treasure.

Hughes, of course, never learned of the new location of the treasure because Hunt and Grounds never returned. Seven months later, March 19, 1882, the two men emerged from hiding on and rode into Charleston, Arizona. Despite having all the stolen loot buried at a location only they knew about, they tried to rob the Tombstone Mining and Milling Company. The robbery attempt turned disastrous. Grounds got killed. Hunt sustained a gunshot wound and was hospitalized. According to one account, he later contracted gangrene. On his deathbed, he sketched a map to the buried treasure and gave it to his uncle, specifying it could be found "at the foot of Davis Mountain."

No such mountain ever existed.

FIFTEEN

BLOOD THIRSTY LYNCH MOB

THE MOB GATHERED OUTSIDE THE SHAWNEE COUNTY JAIL IN TOPEKA, KANSAS, ON THE NIGHT OF JUNE 4, 1889, AND GREW LARGER AND ANGRIER WITH EACH PASSING HOUR, DEMANDING VENGEANCE AGAINST A MAN WHO KILLED A POPULAR AND WELL-RESPECTED LOCAL TAILOR.

Thirty-two year old Nat Oliphant traveled to Topeka to stage several burglaries. The *Daily Capital* described him as "a tough looking individual with sandy complexion, light brown hair, close cropped sideburns and a face that had not seen a razor in days." Just before sunrise, between three and four in the morning on a Tuesday, Oliphant entered the home of Alonzo T. Rodgers through an unlocked glass door from the screened-in back porch. Carrying a .38 caliber revolver, Oliphant made his way to the second floor where Rodgers, his wife, Malvina, and their two young children, were sleeping.

Rodgers, 43, rose when thought he heard a noise coming from one of his daughter's bedrooms. When he stepped out of the bedroom to cross the hallway, he collided with Oliphant in the dark. In a panic, Oliphant fired his revolver and the bullet drilled Rodgers in the stomach. Malvina, his wife, heard the commotion, got up, and hurried to the door. When she saw her husband grappling with another man, she grabbed Oliphant but, according to news accounts, he shot her in the stomach too.

The two shots brought Swedish servant, Mary Klinkerman, who saw Malvina struggling with the burglar to get his gun. Klinkerman grabbed the pistol and tried to wrench it from his grip. Malvina, in the meantime, bit Oliphant on the back of the right hand, and he released the gun. Oliphant broke free of the two women, raced down the steps, and out the door. After a brief manhunt, authorities found him by a Tecumseh railroad bridge, took him into custody, and locked him in a jail cell. Rodgers wouldn't make it because of all the internal bleeding. He died peacefully around 9:30 that morning. His wife survived the gunshot wound she sustained. News of Rodger's death spread quickly through the community.

"This affair is the most frightful that has occurred in the history of Topeka. Here in this quiet city a man universally esteemed, having not an enemy, such was the kindness of his character, is awakened from sleep and in cold blood murdered before his wife and children." —Editorial, *Topeka Daily Capital*

The lynch mob at the jail grew to 15,000, nearly half of Topeka's population of 31,007. Vigilantes helped whip the crowd into a bloodthirsty frenzy. Most doubted the state would execute Oliphant. Between 1872 and 1907, governors refused to sign death warrants for everyone who received death sentences. Inside the jail, authorities listened to the growing anger with concern, but were helpless to do much about it.

"Hang him," someone shouted.

"Bring the rope," another implored.

The police chief, sheriff, and several officers and deputies tried to turn back the lynch mob, but failed and sustained injuries in the scuffle. Ripping the cell door from its hinges, someone looped a rope around Oliphant's shoulders. The mob dragged him down the stairs into the street packed with outraged Topekans. A few men carried Oliphant the steps of the First National Bank building and across the street to a telegraph pole and hanged him.

"An instant later Nat Oliphant was dangling in mid-air," reported The *Daily Capital*. "He was nervy to the last and while there was a shadow of repentance in his expression there was not the slightest tinge of fear. One convulsive movement was made when he had hung about three minutes; that was the last. Someone in the crowd fired a bullet into the body as he swayed to and fro. In mercy and humanity it may be hoped it ended his miserable existence."

The Oliphant lynching was Topeka's last.

SIXTEEN

LAST OF THE STAGECOACH ROBBERS

THE TWO ROBBERS, A MAN AND A WOMAN, WAITED IN HIDING FOR THE BENSON–GLOBE EXPRESS STAGECOACH AT A WATERING POINT NEAR CANE SPRINGS CANYON, ON THE AFTERNOON OF MAY 30, 1899.

Despite the emergence of the railroad as the preferred means of transportation, a few stagecoach lines still covered the remote regions of Arizona Territory. Wielding a six-gun, Pearl Hart stepped out to greet the arriving stage and forced the driver to stop. Wearing a wide-brimmed hat and men's clothing, the five-foot tall Hart ordered the driver down and disarmed him. Joe (or John) Boot, approached the stage from behind with a .45 caliber in hand, motioned the three passengers outside. While Hart kept the foursome in her gun sights, Boot took $5 from a Chinese passenger, $36 from the second passenger, and $390 from a traveling salesman, along with three guns and a gold watch. Minutes later, the bandits rode off.

The hold-up, often mistakenly referred to as the last stagecoach robbery in the United States, had not been well planned. Hart and Boot headed into the wilderness of the Superstition Mountains and wandered around lost. The campfire they built on the third night made it easy for Sheriff William Truman and his posse to find them. They were taken into custody at Poston's Butte, and escorted to Florence.

According to the June 5, 1899, issue of The *New York Times*, "When they were awakened the man seemed paralyzed with fright, but the woman, reaching for the guns, which had been removed, sprang to her feet and fought vigorously."

Since the Florence jail couldn't cater to women prisoners, Hart was transferred to Pima County Jail in Tucson to await trial. By the next morning, the jailer discovered she escape by cutting a hole through a thin partition. Boot, ironically, also managed to vanish from his Florence jail cell. After a couple of weeks on the run, both were re-captured near Deming, New Mexico.

Born Pearl Taylor in 1871 in Lindsay, Ontario, Canada, she eloped at seventeen with gambler Frederick Hart. In 1893, they traveled to Chicago to work at the Columbian Exposition. Hart, the husband, was said to be abusive, couldn't hold his liquor, and squandered away most of their money. Pearl ended up leaving him and went to Colorado where she gave birth to a son. She returned to Ontario and left the child with her parents and then traveled to Phoenix, where she worked as a laundress and cook.

A couple of years later, she and her husband reunited and had a second child. This time, Frederick decided he'd rather be on his own. He left in 1898 to join the Rough Riders and headed off to war, his fate unknown. Pearl, at this point, also left the second child with her parents. Pearl returned to Arizona and eventually met Boot. Both needed a way to make some quick cash, which is when they decided to rob the stagecoach.

Although she admitted her guilt during her trial, jurors apparently were touched by her story that she committed the crime only so should could send money to her ailing mother. He lawyer pointed out it was her first offense. The jury acquitted her. The decision angered Judge Fletcher Doan who claimed she cajoled jurors, "bending them to her will." Doan impaneled a new jury and put her on trial for unlawfully carrying a weapon. The new jury found her guilty within ten minutes. She was sentenced to five years in Yuma Territorial Prison.

In a separate trial, Boot was deemed guilty and sentenced to the same facility, but for a period of thirty years. The prison wasn't built to accommodate female prisoners and Hart was pardoned on December 19, 1902. She moved to Kansas City and starred in a play her sister wrote called *The Arizona Bandit*, but it flopped and she reverted to her old ways. She was arrested and briefly jailed for purchasing stolen canned goods. Little is known about hart's later life. She made a nostalgic trip to Arizona in 1924 to visit the courtroom where she was convicted. It's believed she died sometime after 1928.

Boot, her partner in crime, became a prison trusty and earned the job of driving supply wagons to chain gangs outside the prison walls. On one of those delivery runs, Boot headed for freedom. He had served only two years of his sentence, and was never seen again.

SEVENTEEN

JACK MCCALL'S JOURNEY TO ETERNITY

THE WHISKEY TASTED WATERED-DOWN, BUT THAT DIDN'T KEEP
THE YOUNG MAN WITH THICK CHESTNUT HAIR AND A STUBBY
NOSE FROM KNOCKING BACK DRINK-AFTER-DRINK.

At the bar of Nuttal & Mann's #10 Saloon stood 25-year old Jack
McCall, his attention focused on a nearby card game. When one of
the players pushed back from the corner table and left, McCall—
who went by the name *Bill Sutherland*— stumbled over and took
his place. Across from him sat a handsome, well-built, broad-shouldered man with a large drooping mustache. James Butler *Wild
Bill* Hickok wore two ivory-handled Navy Colt revolvers strapped
to his waist, butts forward.

Too many whiskeys and the oppressive heat of an August afternoon worked against Jack McCall. He sat down with $110 in his
pocket. A short time later, he was broke, losing it all to the man

with the droopy moustache. Wild Bill gathered in his winnings, but pushed some of the money toward McCall, suggesting he use it to get something to eat.

"And, it might be a good idea not to play again until you can cover your losses," he told the drunken McCall. McCall didn't say anything. He scooped up the money and left, anger chipping away at his embarrassment. To his way of thinking, Wild Bill's gesture and advice was no less than condescending.

The details of John "Jack" McCall's background are scant. He was born 1852 or 1853 in Jefferson County, Kentucky, and reared with three sisters. He eventually traveled westward in his late teens and became a buffalo hunter in the Kansas-Nebraska border region around 1869. For a while, he also worked as a laborer and freighter. After spending some time roaming the cattle and railroad towns of Kansas, Nebraska, and Colorado in the early 1870s, he drifted into Wyoming and may have been involved in cattle rustling. News of the gold rush may have lured him to the Black Hills and the gold mining camp of Deadwood. Although McCall was also known as "Crooked Nose Jack" or "Broken Nose Jack," he decided to use the alias *Bill Sutherland* when he arrived in Deadwood.

On August 2, 1876, the day after McCall lost all his money to Hickok, he returned to the saloon about 4 p.m. and ordered a drink at the bar. Wild Bill had arrived a few minutes before and was invited to join Charles Rich, Carl Mann, and Frank Massie in a poker game. Just before he sat down, Hickok asked Rich, who had the chair with his back to the wall, to change places with him. Rich refused. Hickok, who always sat with his back to the wall, conceded and decided to stay. He ordered a *Stone Fence*—a shot of rye in a glass of lemonade—and began playing. McCall moved down the bar, drew an old Colt .45, stepped behind Hickok and fired a shot into his head.

"Damn you, take that," he shouted. The bullet tore through the gunfighter's skull, out his right cheek, and into Massie's forearm; he was sitting opposite Hickok. According to Bill O'Neal in *Encyclopedia of Western Gunfighters,* a later examination of McCall's gun revealed it "was loaded with five defective bullets and only one good cartridge—the one that killed Hickok." McCall, gun in hand, backed toward the door voicing empty threats, ran outside, and leaped on someone's horse nearby. But, the saddle cinch snapped, throwing him to the ground. McCall scrambled to his feet and ran away on foot. He was apprehended a short time later, hiding in a butcher shop.

A miner's court convened the next morning in McDaniel's Theater, but the trial had no legal standing since Deadwood was not part of the Dakota Territory or associated with any jurisdiction in the United States. McCall testified that Hickok killed his brother while in Kansas. He was found not guilty and advised to leave town, which he did, and headed back to Wyoming. Along the journey, however, McCall felt the need to boast of killing Wild Bill Hickok. When authorities got wind of his bragging, McCall was taken into custody on August 29 and taken to Yankton, Dakota Territory. In October, he was indicted for murder, and eventually sentenced to hang.

On the morning of March 1, 1877, McCall stood in the gallows in Yankton. At 10:15, the spring-loaded trap door snapped open. Next stop: Eternity.

Speculation always revolved around why McCall killed Hickok. Being cleaned out by the famed gunfighter may have very well been the motivation. At one point, while in custody, he contended that Deadwood gambler John Varnes paid him to kill Wild Bill. But Varnes couldn't be located. He also tried to implicate another man, who also happened to disappear from Deadwood. McCall's story about Hickok killing his brother was a phony because he never had a brother.

Author Bill O'Neal also wrote that during McCall's trial in Yankton, he was asked why he shot Hickok from behind rather than facing him like a man. McCall replied: "I didn't want to commit suicide."

EIGHTEEN

BUTCH CASSIDY'S
FIRST BANK JOB

ON THE AFTERNOON OF JUNE 24, 1889, THREE MEN RODE INTO TELLURIDE, COLORADO, AND MADE THEIR WAY TO THE SAN MIGUEL VALLEY BANK.

They weren't masked, but wore garish outfits—"five-gallon hats, red bandanas, flashy shirts, chaps and high-heeled cowboy boots" and spurs. Their horses were outfitted in silver-studded bridles and saddles. The idea was to convey the impression they were just cowboys out for a day on the town. While one of the men, Tom McCarty, stayed with the horses, the other two entered the bank. It was around noon on a Monday. Matt Warner walked to the teller's cage to cash a check, while Butch Cassidy took a position a few feet away.

When the teller leaned over to verify the check, Warner clamped his hand around the bank employee's neck, drew his gun, and jammed it against the man's nose. Cassidy, in the meantime, began ransacking the bank and scooped up about $20,000 before he finished. Some accounts of the robbery tell of a possible fourth man being involved who assisted the trio by setting up the relay horses used in the getaway.

Money in-hand, the trio mounted up, and raced for the distant Mancos Mountains. Along the way, they came across Harry Adist, who owned a ranch where Cassidy and Warner recently worked. Later on, when a posse pursuing the robbers spotted Adist, he told them where the outlaws were headed. Warner said the encounter with Adist, although supposedly innocent, proved a point of no return. "It give 'em a clue so they could trace for thousands of miles and for years," he said. "Right at that point is where we broke with our half-outlaw, burned our bridges behind us, and no way to live except by robbing and stealing."

The San Miguel robbery was Cassidy's first major crime. Its success ignited his desire for further scores. Cassidy, born George Leroy Parker, April 13, 1866, in Beaver, Utah, was the eldest of thirteen children of a poor Mormon family. After leaving home as a teen-ager in search of a better lifestyle than the one at home, he worked at different ranches, including one owned by Mike Cassidy. Although the rancher was suspected of stealing cattle and horses, young George Parker admired him. In an effort to emulate his friend and save his family from possible embarrassment, Parker changed his name to *Butch Cassidy*.

In 1890, he bought a ranch in Dubois, Wyoming. The new responsibility, however, didn't keep him from rustling livestock. Four years later, he got caught and went to jail for two years. After his release from prison, Cassidy resumed his life of crime. He joined up with Harry Longabaugh (the Sundance Kid), William Ellsworth Lay (Elzy Lay), Harvey Logan (Kid Curry), Ben Kilpatrick (Tall Texan), Laura Bullion, and others, to form the infamous *Wild Bunch*.

Over the next several years, the Wild Bunch robbed banks and trains and successfully eluded large-scale manhunts. Pursing the gang was difficult because, after each robbery, they would split up and head in different directions, eventually reuniting at a predetermined location, such as the Hole-in-the-Wall hideout in Wyoming or Robber's Roost in southeastern Utah.

Cassidy and Longabaugh, along with Etta Place, left the country in 1901. They ended up in Argentina, lived on a ranch for a few years, and resumed their law-breaking way of life in South America. Bolivian authorities caught up with them in 1908 and reportedly shot them to death. Some, however, believe they escaped and returned to the U.S. where they lived out their lives under new identities.

NINETEEN

A LESSON
NOT LEARNED

A WIRE FENCE, ABOUT SHOULDER-HIGH, BORDERED BOTH SIDES OF
A LONG WALKWAY, GUIDING OUTLAW BEN KILPATRICK TO FREE-
DOM FROM BEHIND THE WALLS OF THE FEDERAL PENITENTIARY
IN ATLANTA, GEORGIA.

When the main door of the sprawling complex opened at about
noon, Tuesday, March 12, 1912, Kilpatrick walked out, almost ten
years to the day he first arrived. The day was pleasant and sunny.
Temperatures lingered in the fifties. A decade behind bars didn't
much change Ben Kilpatrick. While his view of life consisted of little more than 300 acres, the world outside the prison walls under-
went dramatic change.

The *Tall Texan*, as he was known, stood six-foot-two, born on
January 5, 1874, in Coleman, Texas, the third of nine siblings. Not
much information exists about his growing-up years. Historians say

Kilpatrick worked as a cowboy for a while before joining up with Tom "Black Jack" Ketchum's gang. In 1900, he began riding with the Wild Bunch. The gang achieved a reputation as one of the most notorious train robbers on the American frontier. The next year, on July 3, 1901, Kilpatrick and two other members of the Wild Bunch robbed the Great Northern train near Wagner, Montana, and made off with cash and bank notes.

The bandits split up, as they always did. Kilpatrick and girl-friend, *Laura Bullion*, also a member of the Wild Bunch, headed to St. Louis, Missouri. On November 5th, they were arrested for trying to pass forged and stolen bank notes. Bullion got a five-year sentence, and served three-and-one-half years of it. Kilpatrick, on the other hand, received fifteen years at hard labor for passing forged notes and for train robbery. The Tall Texan went to the Ohio State Penitentiary and, in 1905, transferred to the federal prison in Atlanta.

After leaving prison, Kilpatrick wasn't aware how much times had changed, and went back to the only way he knew of collecting income: Crime. He staged a series of train and bank robberies, but the stolen loot never amounted to enough to prevent him from continuing his dangerous line of work. On March 12, 1912—or the day after—Kilpatrick and a partner boarded a Southern Pacific express train near Sanderson, Texas.

During the robbery, he forced his way into the mail car. Wells Fargo clerk, David Trousdale, retaliated and clubbed Kilpatrick several times with a wooden ice mallet and killed him.

TWENTY

MOURNING
IN DELTA

ON A QUIET SATURDAY MORNING, SEPTEMBER 7, 1893, A FATHER AND SON WALKED INTO THE FARMERS & MERCHANTS BANK IN DELTA, COLORADO, PULLED THEIR PISTOLS AND DEMANDED MONEY.

The leader of the gang, Tom McCarty, waited with the horses in an alley at the rear of the bank. Inside the bank, Bill McCarty and teen-age son Fred, ordered co-founder and cashier Andrew Blachly to hand over the cash. Blachly, a father of eight, was well-liked in the community. He resisted the younger McCarty's order and shouted for help. Panicked, the younger McCarty squeezed the trigger twice, killing the 46-year old with a shot to the head. When Tom McCarty heard the shooting, he mounted up and rode off.

The two gunmen inside the bank snatched whatever cash they could and bolted out the back door to their horses and headed north. When Delta citizens heard the gunfire, they headed for the bank, armed and angry at word of the cold-blooded killing. Across the street at W.G. Simpson & Son Hardware, Ray Simpson sat at the front of the store cleaning his rifle, a Sharps .44 caliber. When he heard the shooting, Simpson chambered a shell, left the store and ran down Third Street to the alley intersecting the bank. According to one account, the two bank robbers spotted Simpson and fired at him. The hardware merchant, with a reputation as a sharpshooter, took aim and returned fire. The first bullet blew the top of Bill McCarty's forehead away.

Witnesses say the outlaw's son, Fred, reined his horse to a stop, possibly with the thought of helping his father. The maneuver proved fatal. Simpson fired again, hitting the young man in the temple. Most of the money was recovered. Tom McCarty, for the most part, vanished from the pages of history after the botched robbery in Delta. Some say he made several threats about return-ing to kill the man who killed his brother and nephew, but never followed through. Historians believe he was killed in a gunfight in Bitterroot, Montana, in 1900.

Although the bank building was turned into a home and moved, Blachly's eight orphaned sons—in 1958—placed a plaque at the bank site to commemorate the tragedy.

TWENTY-ONE

BAD DAYS
OF ZIP WYATT

ON A QUIET THURSDAY IN MARCH 1894, THREE MEN WALKED INTO THE BLAINE COUNTY GENERAL STORE IN TODD, OKLAHOMA, PISTOLS IN HAND. INSIDE, THE OWNER AND HIS FAMILY WERE BUSY STOCKING SHELVES AND CLEANING THE PLACE.

E.H. Townsend looked up and found himself facing three armed outlaws. After he watched Zip Wyatt, the leader of the trio, rifle the money drawer, Townsend tried to bar the door so they couldn't leave. One of the gunmen shot Townsend in the wrist. But the wound didn't stop him. Still holding the bar, he whipped it around and knocked Wyatt to the floor. The other two men both fired at the same time, killing Townsend, with wife and children looking on.

Born Nathaniel Ellsworth Wyatt, in 1863 to an Indiana farm family, he and his brother headed for Oklahoma in 1889. His brother Nim, also known as Six-Shooter Jack, got killed in a bar in Texline, Texas. Historians say Wyatt turned bad after his brother's death. He started his crime spree by shooting up the town of Mulhall, Oklahoma, on June 3, 1891, and wounding two citizens. When authorities issued a warrant for his arrest, he fled to Kansas and Kiowa County. A month later, he stole riding gear, and he was on the run again.

Deputy Sheriff Andrew Balfour picked up Wyatt's trail and tracked him to Pryor's Grove, Kansas, on July 4th. When he tried to make an arrest, Wyatt shot him in the stomach. Balfour, suffering from a severe wound, managed to return fire and hit Wyatt twice in the hand, but the wounds weren't serious. Balfour died, leaving a wife and six children. With a $1,000 reward on his head, Wyatt made his way back to Indiana to lie low for a while. He got arrested there and was returned to Oklahoma and jailed in Guthrie. He managed to escape twice, the second time on New Year's Eve 1892.

Wyatt resumed his life of crime under the aliases Zip, Wild Charlie, and Dick Yaeger. He held up merchants, post offices, and trains, never hesitating to use his gun. Some contend Wyatt may have killed as many as eleven people. Less than a month after robbery and killing in Todd, Wyatt struck again. This time, the victim was Dewey County Treasurer Fred Hoffman.

In May, Wyatt and his gang boarded the Santa Fe train at Whorton, Oklahoma. When the station agent tried to telegraph an urgent message for help, Wyatt gunned him down. Wyatt formed a gang with outlaw Ike Black and staged another series of robberies and killings. On August 1, 1895, the gang got in a shootout and lawmen killed Black. Wyatt, although wounded, slipped away again. Three days later, a posse cornered him at Skeleton Creek and engaged in another shootout. Wyatt went down with a gut shot and a shattered pelvis. He held on until after midnight on September 7 and died. His body was never claimed. One account says his sister showed up to gather his personal belongings, but refused to claim the body. The sheriff denied her request.

The city put Wyatt in a pauper's grave south of Enid, dead at age 32.

TWENTY-TWO

THE
LONG MANHUNT

A LOW MIST FLOATED OVER THE OUACHITA RIVER AS LAWMEN TRAMPED THROUGH THE DARK, MURKY SWAMPLAND OF MOUNT IDA, ARKANSAS, HUNTING FOR THE MAN WHO KILLED THE SHER-IFF OF BAXTER COUNTY.

On Saturday, September 4, 1897, the five-year pursuit came to an end when a posse finally corralled Jesse B. Roper. The killer had succeeded in evading the law at every turn. Before authorities learned of this location, Roper already spent several months hiding in the swamplands with his dog and a Winchester his only companions. He killed Sheriff A.G. Byler while trying to avoid arrest for an indictment charging him with unlawfully carrying a firearm. Byler and a posse showed up at the ranch where the Georgia-born Roper was staying with relatives. Roper, hiding behind the corner of an outbuilding, braced his rifle against his shoulder and took aim. When Sheriff Byler dismounted, the gunman fired. Roper, an expert marksman, only needed one shot. Byler fell to the ground dead, at 63. And, Roper fled on foot.

Byler served as Baxter County's first sheriff from 1872 to 1884, and also from 1890 to 1892. A well-respected member of the community, Byler was among the county's first settlers, according to the *Baxter Bulletin*. Born in Trigg County, Kentucky in 1853, Byler, worked as a farmer and tanner. The owner of a large tannery, Byler invested in all the cattle hides he could get, then sold the leather to settlers to make shoes.

Before pinning on a badge, Byler served in the Civil War, helping drill Confederate troops preparing for battle. He was a popular sheriff and served four consecutive terms. Taking a break from law enforcement, he represented the county as a state legislator. After a couple of terms, he ran again for sheriff and won two more terms.

A $1,500 reward was posted for the capture of the 26-year old Roper. Additional allegations involving the murders of a cattle inspector in Nebraska, a man in New Mexico, and bank robbery, pushed the total reward money to nearly $4,500. Roper's fate was as murky as the swampland where authorities found him hiding. According to an article in the *Bulletin*, Roper killed two fellow prisoners in a jail in Lufkin, Texas, in August 1906, and then committed suicide, hanging himself in his cell with a section he ripped from a blanket. But, in the *History of Baxter County*, a historian agreed that Roper committed suicide, but not until twelve years later—1918—in an *Oklahoma* jail cell while awaiting trial on yet another charge.

Distant relatives in Georgia accused newspapers of sensationalizing anything to do with Roper, and insisted that no one really knew how Roper met his fate.

TWENTY-THREE

A MATTER OF LAW
OR DISORDER

ALTHOUGH HE WORE A BADGE, A *COMMITMENT* TO LAW AND ORDER WAS NEVER A CONCEPT DEPUTY SHERIFF CHARLEY ALLISON EMBRACED.

In some ways, Allison was no different than many other law-men of the 19th century. The deputy sheriff of Conejos County, Colorado, worked both sides when it came to law and order. Allison was no ordinary outlaw. At five-eight, he trained and once worked as a railroad engineer. For the most part, he stands as a mystery in the Old West. Dark complexioned, with gray eyes, Allison was born *Charles Annis* in Virginia. Some say others easily influenced him. The only sure conclusion about him was that he wasn't committed to either breaking the law, or enforcing it.

When Allison lost total interest in enforcing the law, he decided to organize a gang of outlaws to rob stagecoaches between Colorado and New Mexico. In fact, he spent most of his career robbing stage-coaches. The gang pulled five armed stagecoach robberies around Alamosa, Colorado. Then, it headed to Amargo, New Mexico, and established camp on the outskirts of the tent city, home to a community of railroad workers. From the new encampment, Allison's outlaws proceeded to terrorize the countryside. The highwaymen spent most of their time drinking, playing cards, and sleeping, and left their tents only to rob and plunder.

Among the favored targets: newly-arriving passengers of the Denver & Rio Grande Railroad that connected Chama, New Mexico, to Durango, Colorado. The crime spree came to an end in 1881 when Sheriff Matt Kyle arrested Allison. He was convicted on Oct. 21st. The next day, a judge sentenced him to a jail term of thirty-four years. Later, the governor commuted the sentence of "Prisoner number 646" and he was released in 1890.

TWENTY-FOUR

THE LAST DESPERADO

ON AN EARLY WEDNESDAY MORNING, JUNE 9, 1902, TWO PRISONERS ESCAPED FROM THE OREGON STATE PENITENTIARY. ONE OF THEM KILLED GUARDS AND CIVILIANS BEFORE MAKING THEIR WAY TO FREEDOM.

The prisoners, Harry Tracy and David Merrill, entered the prison foundry building about 7 a.m. with a work detail and retrieved weapons smuggled in by an accomplice from the outside. Armed with rifles and pistols, Tracy and Merrill shot their way to freedom. On their way over the wall, they left behind the dead bodies of three guards and three civilians and a wounded inmate. The bloody prison break triggered one of the greatest manhunts in the waning days of the Old West.

Born Harry Severns, in Pittsville, Wisconsin in 1874, he started riding the outlaw trail early in life. He headed west to Oregon and began a life of crimes, arrests, convictions, and jailbreaks. Tracy wasn't all that adept at breaking the law and got caught several times. But he was able to outwit most of the lawmen who pursued him. He finally got arrested for the murder of cattle rancher V.S. Hoy and put behind bars at the Routt County Jail in Colorado. But he got the best of the sheriff, administered a severe beating, and escaped. He also managed to break out of the Utah Penitentiary.

In 1898, Tracy returned to Portland, Oregon. He met David Merrill, another common criminal, and they became partners in crime. Between crimes, Tracy married Merrill's sister, Rose. The two men celebrated their new partnership by robbing merchants in downtown Portland. Various accounts of their escapades suggest that both men were members of the Hole-in-the-Wall gang based in Utah—not the one associated with Butch Cassidy and the Sundance Kid.

The law caught up to Tracy and Merrill and they ended up in the Oregon State Pen. Tracy received a twenty-year sentence. Merrill got twelve years. After their prison break, Tracy and Merrill headed north, trying to put distance between them and a contingent of about 250 lawmen. After crossing the Columbia River into Washington, they stopped for a meal at a cabin owned by a farmer near Vancouver.

Tracy noticed a copy of the *Oregonian* newspaper. While glancing through it, he saw a story about Merrill's mother. According to the report, she turned in the two men, but only after assurances that her son would receive a shorter sentence than Tracy's. Tracy always wondered why he received a harsher sentence than Merrill when they were convicted in Oregon. Now, he knew. Upon reach Chehalis, Tracy confronted Merrill with the information and ultimately shot his brother-in-law in the back, killing him.

A posse finally caught up to Tracy at a small farmhouse outside Creston, Washington, where he was hiding and tried to make a break for it. In the ensuing gun battle, he took two bullets in the leg, one of them shattering a major artery. Losing a considerable amount of blood, Tracy crawled through a field of waist-high wheat. Once, he promised no one would ever take him alive. He carried through on the vow by putting his revolver under his right eye and squeezing the trigger, killing himself.

The July 3, 1902, issue of the *Seattle Daily Times* stated that, "In all the criminal lore of the country there is no record equal to that of Harry Tracy for cold-blooded nerve, desperation and thirst for crime. Jesse James, compared with Tracy, is a Sunday school teacher."

TWENTY-FIVE

JIM BERRY'S FATAL MISTAKE

J IM BERRY RODE INTO MEXICO, MISSOURI, ON OCTOBER 5, 1877, FLUSH WITH CASH, HIS SHARE OF THE LOOT TAKEN IN A TRAIN ROBBERY AT BIG SPRINGS, NEBRASKA.

Less than a month before, he and five other members of the Black Hills Bandits staged the biggest single robbery in history of the Union Pacific Railroad. The gang split $60,000 in newly minted twenty-dollar gold pieces and went their separate ways. He stayed the night in the community of Mexico. On Saturday morning, before leaving for the family farm in Callaway County, Berry lugged his heavy saddlebags to three different banks to get the $9,000 in gold coins converted to paper currency.

Berry's impatience proved a fatal mistake. The banks, as customary, shipped the coins to a depository in St. Louis. On Monday, after receiving word the coins probably came from the Big Springs

77

railroad robbery, the banks contacted authorities. The next morning, railroad detectives arrived to meet Audrain County Sheriff Henry Glasscock and traveled to nearby Callaway County. The trio searched Berry's home, but couldn't find him. A few days later, the hunt ended when a posse tracked the outlaw to a hiding place in the woods, about a mile from the family farm. The two sides exchanged gunfire. Berry tried to escape. But, Sheriff Glassock brought him down with a shotgun blast, wounding him eight times in the left leg.

Glasscock escorted the prisoner back to Mexico, Missouri, and sent for a doctor. When Berry recovered, the sheriff planned to transport him to authorities in Omaha, Nebraska. Monday night, however, Berry's condition worsened. Gangrene set in. The infection, coupled with the loss of blood, put him at death's door. Before he died, Berry talked about the train robbery. The *Mexico Weekly Ledger* reported that Berry admitted to the Union Pacific heist, and in the presence of several witnesses. According to the newspaper, Berry "said he was not sorry for it...He would say nothing about those of the gang who are yet alive." He died the next day. The outlaw was 39.

A few hours before Berry took his last breath, his elderly mother died. He was buried next to his mother outside Shamrock, Missouri. Detectives recovered $2,840 from Berry, but never determined what happened to the rest of the cash.

TWENTY-SIX

LAME JOHNNY'S LAST RIDE

FIVE GUNMEN HIDING INSIDE THE STAGE STATION AT CANYON SPRINGS, SOUTH DAKOTA, WAITED FOR THE ARRIVAL OF THE *MONITOR*, A SPECIAL IRONCLAD TREASURE COACH.

Owned by the Homestake Mine in the Black Hills, the *Monitor* carried large quantities of precious metals. The coach was covered with 5/16" iron plate and modified with portholes for guns. Inside the treasure box bolted to the floor were three gold ingots worth about $10,000, several ounces of gold dust and nuggets valued at about $14,530, $1,000 in diamonds and jewelry, and around $2,000 in currency. When the *Monitor* approached the station at mid-afternoon, Thursday, September 26, 1878, the gunmen opened fire, killing one of the messenger guards and wounding two others.

Cornelius Donahue served as leader of the gang—a well-dressed, well-mannered young man otherwise known as *Lame*

Johnny. He walked with a limp, probably from an injury during childhood. Lame Johnny came from Philadelphia. He was born about 1850, and attended Girard College. After the Civil War, he decided to head west to work at a ranch in Texas where he learned the finer points of stealing horses. News of the gold rush took him to the Black Hills. He tried prospecting for a while, but gave it up and took a job with Homestake Mine as a bookkeeper, going by the alias of John Hurley. He left the job after someone recognized him as a horse thief from Texas.

Lame Johnny resumed his criminal career of cattle rustling and horse thievery, and then robbing stagecoaches. At Canyon Springs, once the gang overpowered the *Monitor* guards, they spent about two hours prying open the treasure box with sledgehammers and chisels. After they divvied up the loot, Lame Johnny and the other gang members split up. When news of the stagecoach heist reached Deadwood, about 37 miles away, a posse was organized and left to pursue the gang. The Cheyenne and Black Hills stage line offered a reward of $2,500 "for the return of the money and valuables" and conviction of the five men who robbed the stage.

During the next several weeks, four of the gang members were captured and eventually lynched by vigilantes. About sixty-percent of the stolen loot was recovered. Lame Johnny, easily recognized by his limp, was caught at the Pine Ridge Reservation, taken to Chadron, Nebraska, where he was put on a stage for Deadwood. He was shackled and handcuffed to a metal plate fastened to the floor.

About eight miles north of Buffalo Cap in Dakota Territory, a group of masked vigilantes stopped the stage, pried Lame Johnny loose from the floorboard, and dragged him to an elm tree where they hanged him, shackles still attached. The next morning, a group of freighters found Lame Johnny, cut him down and buried him under the tree. The rest of the stolen shipment was never recovered.

TWENTY-SEVEN

PETTICOAT TERROR
OF THE PLAINS

THE UNKNOWN ASSASSIN WAITED AS THE WOMAN ON HORSE-
BACK RODE TOWARD HER CABIN AT YOUNGER'S BEND ON THE
CANADIAN RIVER, NEAR EUFAULA, OKLAHOMA.

When she drew closer, the gunman stepped out from his hiding place with a shotgun and fired. The blast slammed into her back, throwing her from the saddle. Struggling, she tried to stand up, but a second shot finished her. Belle Starr—wife, mistress, mother, and horse thief—lay in the roadway, dead at age forty. Her violent death took place on February 3, 1889, while returning from a ride to Fort Smith. No one was ever charged in the ambush, but fingers pointed to several suspects.

Among them was Edgar Watson, one of her sharecroppers. Starr threatened to turn Watson over to the law as an escaped murderer from Florida. Watson was arrested but acquitted for lack of evidence. Some believe her husband, Jim July, who also went by the name of Jim July Starr, killed Belle because of a bitter argument over an affair he was having. Suspicion also fell on her own son, Ed Reed. She, reportedly, had whipped her son for mistreating one of her horses. Rumors persisted that she forced her son into an incestuous affair. Some historians, however, discount him as a suspect. They said the two hadn't seen each other in months and he lived miles from her.

Myra Belle Shirley—later known as Belle Starr—was born in Carthage, Missouri, the daughter of a successful innkeeper. Her mother, Elizabeth "Hatfield" Shirley descended from Hatfields, part of the infamous Hatfield-McCoy family feud, that took place in the West Virginia-Kentucky region. The parents sent their daughter to Missouri's Carthage Female Academy, a private institution, where she studied and excelled in the classics. Despite being an educated woman, Belle Starr felt more comfortable in saloons, drinking and gambling. Dressed in high-topped boots, skirts, she wore a man's Stetson topped off with an ostrich plume. She also sported twin-holstered pistols. The family moved to Sycene, Texas, in 1864, a few miles from Dallas. Some say that, as a teenager, Belle helped the Confederacy by reporting the positions of Union troops.

Starr supposedly had a brief fling with Cole Younger, a member of the James Gang, which sometimes used the Shirley farm as a hideout. It was about then, she began flirting with a life of crime. While working as a dealer in a Dallas gaming hall, Belle met and married James Reed in 1866, and the couple had a daughter. When Reed was accused of cattle rustling, he moved the family to California where Belle gave birth to a son. Family life, however, didn't change Reed. Accused of counterfeiting, Reed, Belle, and the two kids returned to Texas. He and Belle supported their new family by stealing horses and robbing people. Following Reed's death, Belle entered into several common-law marriages.

She did marry Cherokee Sam Starr in 1880, and lived in Eufaula, Oklahoma.

Her bad-girl conduct got her into trouble with Judge Isaac Parker. And, when she got arrested in 1882 for stealing an $85 horse, Judge Parker sentenced her to a year in a Detroit House of Corrections. Nine months later, she was released and returned home. Sam Starr, her husband, tangled with a lawman and killed each other in a gunfight.

Belle entered into another common-law marriage, this one to Jim July, but she convinced him to change his name to Jim July Starr. Most stories about Belle Starr are laced more with fiction than fact. Her reputation as a so-called bandit queen was somewhat exaggerated. But, fact or fiction, the name of Belle Starr shares the pages of American history with other legends of the West.

TWENTY-EIGHT

TOO EASY TO CATCH

TWO GUNMEN, REVOLVERS DRAWN, FORCED THE STAGECOACH DRIVER TO REIN HIS TEAM TO A STOP NEAR MUDDY STATION, IN CARBON COUNTY, WYOMING.

Stage driver Abraham Coon noticed the two men wore dark suits and heavy overcoats on a cold and windy Sunday afternoon, December 29, 1889. The stagecoach carried one passenger, a man named Allen. According to the driver, each of the robbers wore fake whiskers and mustaches, fashioned from small pieces of buffalo rope, fastened to the back of their ears with strings. The younger of the bandits ordered Coon and his passenger out of the coach. He then retrieved the mailbag from under the seat, sliced through the straps, and emptied it onto the ground. Coon said the gunman opened letters and packages and stuffed some of the contents into his pockets. When he asked Allen how much money he had on him, the passenger handed over a buckskin pouch containing a small amount of cash. He asked Coon the same question.

"About four bits," the driver answered, and invited the outlaw to search him if he didn't believe what he said. According to author Larry Pointer, in his book, *In Search of Butch Cassidy*, the gunman told Coon to keep his money. "No, you can keep that, and when you get into Rawlins drink to the health of Frank Jackson." It's not known whether the bandit used the name as an alias or was referring to a bank robber with the same name who rode with the Sam Bass Gang. With those words, the two robbers rode off.

After reporting the robbery to authorities in Rawlins, Coon learned the two bandits went by the names of William Brown and Tom Ricketts. Several months later, the two men ended up in Moab, Utah. During a community dance they both attended, Brown bragged to someone that he was forced to flee from "up north" because a stage robbery he committed. Word got back to authorities in Wyoming. In September 1890, the pair was arrested and escorted to Wyoming Territorial Penitentiary to await trial. Rickets admitted he was using an alias and admitted his real name was *Dan Sinclair Parker* "of the Parker family in Utah." He provided authorities with the names of all his family members, but neglected to include a brother: Robert Leroy Parker, better known as Butch Cassidy, the notorious leader of the Wild Bunch Gang.

Dan Parker was sentenced to life in prison at the Detroit House of Correction. In 1894, however, the governor of Wyoming pardoned him. He apparently returned to Utah and lived out the rest of his life as a law-abiding citizen. Another version of the story indicated that Dan Parker returned west and tried to join the Wild Bunch. But brother Butch turned him down, saying, "You're too damned easy to catch."

TWENTY-NINE

DAY OF RECKONING

THE TENSION ON THE STREETS OF PAWNEE, OKLAHOMA TERRITORY, WAS THICK AS QUICKSAND WHEN OUTLAW BEE DUNN RODE IN CARRYING NO PRETENSE ABOUT WANTING TO KILL DEPUTY U.S. MARSHAL FRANK M. CANTON.

Bad blood flowed between the two ever since Canton tried, but failed, to arrest Dunn and his brothers on murder charges. He was still hopeful of bringing them to justice for stealing cattle. Canton backed into a career in law enforcement after spending much of his youth on the side of disorder. Born in Virginia in 1849 as Josiah W. "Joe" Horner, the family moved to Texas when he was a teenager. Horner became a cowboy and worked for cattleman Burk Burnett driving herds to railheads in Kansas.

When he turned 22, Horner got into trouble robbing banks and rustling cattle. He also went on the run for killing a Buffalo soldier in a barroom brawl. He was captured after an 1877 bank robbery in Comanche, Texas, but gave Texas Rangers the slip and joined a cattle drive to Ogallala, Nebraska. Vowing to give up the outlaw life, he changed his name to Frank Canton and went to work for the powerful Wyoming Stock Growers Association as a stock detective. He was elected sheriff of Johnson County, Wyoming, in 1882, served four years, and then went back to working for the WSGA.

Canton ranked among the major figures involved in the *Johnson County War* of 1892. Two years later, he moved to Oklahoma Territory, served as undersheriff in Pawnee County, and got appointed deputy U.S. marshal for Judge Isaac Parker. He played a vital role in helping bring the Bill Doolin and other outlaw gangs to justice. Fearing that Dunn would follow through on his pledge to kill Canton on sight, the lawman ignored pleas from friends to leave the county.

On a chilly Friday, November 6, Canton was busy serving court subpoenas when he was told of Dunn's arrival. But he didn't pay much attention. Canton stepped out of a restaurant and started walking up the plank sidewalk toward the courthouse, both hands shoved in his pockets to ward off the chill. Clipped to the waistband of his trousers, above his right hand, was a .45 caliber Colt revolver. He rarely wore a cartridge belt while working in town.

"As I started up the street in a brisk walk, Bee Dunn stepped in front of me," Canton recalled, saying that Dunn threatened him to his face. Dunn stood with his hand on his revolver, but hadn't yet drawn. Canton studied the outlaw, "and I saw murder in his eyes." Wasting no time, Canton drew his .45 and fired. The bullet struck Dunn in the forehead. As he started to fall, Dunn drew the revolver, but it dropped to the sidewalk.

Three decades after the shooting, Canton told a slightly different version. He said when the two locked eyes, Dunn went for his gun, but it got snagged on his suspenders. The brief second of delay gave Canton the advantage. Canton said he was forced to make a headshot because a few days earlier, he learned that a blacksmith had fashioned a steel breastplate for Dunn.

"If I had shot at his body, I wouldn't have killed him and he would have filled me full of lead before I had known what was happening," said Canton.

The following year, Canton joined the gold rush to Alaska, then returned to Oklahoma in 1907 and became adjutant general for the Oklahoma National Guard. At one point, historians say he met with the governor of Texas, admitted to being Joe Horner, and was eventually granted a pardon. He died on September 28, 1927, at age 78.

THIRTY

DARING DAYLIGHT ROBBERY

WHEN JUDGE JAMES SANDUSKY CROSSED COURTHOUSE SQUARE IN LIBERTY, MISSOURI, IN THE EARLY MORNING OF FEBRUARY 13, 1866, HE LOOKED UP AND SAW ABOUT A DOZEN WELL-ARMED MEN, THEIR BREATHS VISIBLE IN THE EARLY MORNING CHILL, RIDE SLOWLY PAST HIM.

Three of the men break off from the group and move to what he later described as strategic positions in the square. The others fanned out in front of Clay County Savings Association. According to several accounts, Frank James and Cole Younger dismounted and entered the bank. Jesse James, Frank's brother, was absent nursing a gunshot wound to the lung that he sustained just before the end of the Civil War.

Inside the bank, Frank James supposedly approached Greenup Bird, who stood behind the counter, and asked the cashier to change a large bill. Sliding his pistol from the holster, James raised it to Bird's face. Younger drew his own gun, crawled across the counter, and grabbed Bird's son, William, the only other person in the bank. The two employees were then ordered to fill a large grain sack with all the money in the bank. The Greenups poured silver and gold coins into the sack, along with the contents of a tin box that contained currency, bank notes, and bonds. The estimated amount of the robbery stood at between $57,000 and $62,000.

Before escaping, the gunmen pushed the Greenups into the green bank vault, and slammed the door shut. But the vault didn't lock. Father and son shoved the door open, ran to the windows, and began yelling "Robbery!" The gang raced to their horses, gave a Rebel yell, fired into the air several times, and galloped away in triumph because, up to then, no bank in the country had ever been hit in broad daylight during peacetime. Members of the James-Younger Gang, which reportedly included Confederate guerrillas, had been eager to write a new chapter in the battle pitting law against order in the American West. The getaway, however, didn't go as planned, resulting in the killing of a teen-ager. Two young men walking down the street witnessed the commotion and turned to run, but gang member Archie Clement, a compulsive killer, shot down George Wymore, a college student, for no reason at all.

Clement served as a Confederate guerrilla leader in the Civil War and established a reputation for brutality towards Union soldiers and pro-Union civilians in Missouri. In addition to the brutal death of 19-year old Wymore, there were other ramifications to the daring, daylight robbery. The state authorities believed it was Clement who led the raid and issued a reward for his capture. Later, however, the James Gang got most of the blame for the robbery, and similar ones at small-town banks across Missouri in the months ahead.

"I think there were about ten men in the robbery. No one was recognized. I do not remember that they were disguised in any way. I do not

think there was more than suspicion as to who the parties were," said Judge Sandusky, talking about what he remembered of the robbery.

The day after the robbery, fresh snow fell and covered the tracks left by the bank robbers, preventing authorities from tracking them. Along with Confederate guerrillas, Kansas Redlegs were also implicated in the heist. The bank offered a $5,000 reward to anyone who recovered the money.

The robbery triggered a far greater economic consequence than the money that was taken. Clay County Savings Association—now called the Jesse James Bank Museum—ended up closing its doors due to insufficient funds. Depositors received only 60-cents on the dollar.

An amusing story surfaced about an incident that supposedly occurred in later years when Cole Younger and Frank James were traveling with a wild west show using their names and outlaw fame as its main attraction. The two men were reportedly being chauffeured around a town on the tour, reminiscing about their past. Younger apparently suggested they stop at a bank to change some money. Frank paused for a moment, or so, and smiled.

"If Cole Younger and Frank James walk into a bank together, the first thing they'd do is slam the vault shut and start shooting."

The pair decided to send their driver in to get change. Younger, in a memoir he wrote, saw himself more as a Confederate avenger than an outlaw. In fact, he admitted to only one crime: the bank robbery attempt in Northfield, Minnesota, in 1876. On August 21, 1912, Younger declared that he had become a Christian and expressed regret about his criminal past. Frank James died February 18, 1915, and Younger a little over a year later on March 21, 1916.

THIRTY-ONE

THE
HIGH FIVES

O N A SLEEPY TUESDAY AFTERNOON, AUGUST 6, 1895, MOST PEO-
PLE WERE AT LUNCH WHEN FIVE MEN ON HORSEBACK ENTERED
THE BORDER TOWN OF NOGALES, ARIZONA, FOLLOWED THE
RAILROAD TRACKS DOWN DESERTED MORLEY AVENUE, AND MADE
THEIR WAY TO THE FRONT OF INTERNATIONAL BANK.

William *Black Jack*, Christian, the leader of the group, scanned
both sides of the street and gave a quick nod to the others. As
planned, he and George Musgrave—a wanted killer and cattle
rustler—along with Bob Hayes, dismounted and walked inside.
Christian's brother, Bob, and Code Young stayed with the horses.
The Christian brothers were no strangers to crime. Earlier that
summer, they were arrested for killing a police officer in Guthrie,
Oklahoma. They escaped, however, and headed to New Mexico
and Arizona territories where the pair organized a gang called The

High Fives, and began robbing stagecoaches, trains, post offices, small stores, and banks.

Black Jack had learned that International Bank would have between $10,000 and $30,000 cash on hand for an area rancher who planned to close a cattle purchase. Once inside the bank, Black Jack chambered a bullet into his Winchester and pointed it at Major Fred Herrera, the cashier. Musgrave circled the counter, holding bank president John Dessart at gunpoint. Hayes herded others into a back room. While Herrera was busy stuffing money into the feedbag he was handed, Dessart decided to make a break for the door. During the confusion, Herrera grabbed his pistol from beneath the counter and fired, wounding Musgrave in the knee. When the customers and patrons in the back room heard the disturbance, they escaped through a back door.

Black Jack Christian, who retrieved the bag of money, dropped it as he fled through the front door. The foiled robbery alerted other citizens in town and the situation turned ugly for the High Fives. A customs inspector by the name of Frank King, standing across from the bank, sprang into action. He took his gun and began firing. The bullets missed the gang members, but wounded two of the horses. Musgrave, injured and without a horse, managed to swing aboard Black Jack's horse, and the High Fives started riding hard, heading for Mexico. Some distance from town, the men split up.

A few days later, a posse organized by Sheriff Bob Leatherwood of Tucson gave chase, but were ambushed by Bob Christian, Hayes, and Young. During the gunfire, Deputy Frank Robson was killed, and the High Fives escaped. Two years later, however, the gang returned to Arizona Territory and resumed robbing stagecoaches and trains.

Black Jack and his brother Bob, along with Musgrave and his brother, Calvin, and an outlaw named Sid Moore, were using a desolate canyon, about twelve miles from Clifton, as their hideout. On the morning of April 28, 1897, a small posse of five men, headed by Deputy U.S. Marshal Fred R. Higgins of Roswell, New Mexico, spotted the gang as they emerged from the canyon. Shots were exchanged in the early morning shootout and the gang decided to flee, but one of the High Fives didn't make it. The lawmen found Black Jack Christian facedown in the dirt, his body riddled with bullets.

THIRTY-TWO

JOHNNY-BEHIND-THE-DEUCE

THE LIQUOR FLOWED FREELY AS THE HOURS TICKED AWAY DURING AN ALL-NIGHT POKER GAME AT QUINN'S SALOON IN THE ROUGH MILL TOWN OF CHARLESTON, ARIZONA, ON THE WEST BANK OF THE PEDRO RIVER, A FEW MILES SOUTHEAST OF TOMBSTONE.

Around lunchtime on Friday, January 14, 1881, W.P Schneider, chief engineer of the Corbin Mill, decided to call it quits, angry at the heavy losses he suffered. When Schneider pushed his chair back and got up, he hurled an accusation about cheating at one of the players, Michael O'Rourke, a professional gambler known as *Johnny-Behind-the-Deuce*. O'Rourke got slapped with the nickname due to his habit of betting heavily when he held no more than a deuce as his hole-card.

The two men exchanged insults and, according to one bystander, Schneider whipped out a knife. Another story contends he drew a gun. One particular account says the shooting occurred, not over gambling, but because Schneider accused O'Rourke of stealing several items from his home, including clothing. Regardless of the weapon or the story, O'Rourke apparently responded by firing his own pistol, and Schneider fell to the floor, dead, a bullet in his chest.

The engineer was a popular member of the Charleston community. The saloon crowd of miners, cattlemen, and soldiers from nearby Fort Huachuca, included a number of men who worked for Schneider. Tombstone Marshal George McKelvey arrived on the scene and took O'Rourke into custody, placed him in the back of a buckboard, and headed to Tombstone. Back at the saloon, the shooting fanned flames of anger. Outlaws Curly Bill Brocius and John Ringo supposedly whipped the miners into a lynch-happy mob and decided to chase the gambler down and string him to a tree.

A gunshot startled McKelvey and he turned to see the lynch-happy mob in pursuit, not yet within gun range. But the angry riders began closing the distance between them. Just two miles from Tombstone, he heard the bark of rifles and found himself dodging bullets. When the mules reached Jack McCann's Last Chance Saloon, they couldn't continue. Deputy U.S. Marshal Virgil Earp rode up, sized up the situation, and put O'Rourke on his own horse, handing him off to Assistant Marshal Morgan Earp who took the prisoner to Vogan's Bowling Alley. Pima County Deputy Sheriff Wyatt Earp met the lynch mob, armed with his shotgun, and convinced them to disband.

Johnny-Behind-the-Deuce was escorted to a jail in Tucson, charged with murder. He tried to escape in March with seven other prisoners, but the attempt failed. In mid-April, however, O'Rourke succeeded in a second attempt and disappeared. Historians are mixed on the fate of Johnny-Behind-the-Deuce. Some suggest he returned to Charleston, hunted down Johnny Ringo, and killed him near West Turkey Creek. Ringo was found shot to death in a clump of oak trees at the same location, but his death remains unresolved. O'Rourke seems to have vanished—at least from the pages of history.

One report puts the gambler in Sulphur Springs Valley in 1882 where he was again accused of cheating. Another report maintains a friend of Ringo gunned him down. Whatever the case, Johnny-Behind-The-Deuce never stood trial for killing W.P. Schneider in Charleston, Arizona.

THIRTY-THREE

THE RED JACK GANG

A MAN WITH RED HAIR AND A PALE COMPLEXION STOOD IN THE SHADOWS ACROSS FROM THE WELLS FARGO OFFICE IN FLORENCE, ARIZONA, AND WATCHED TWO MEN LIFT A HEAVY EXPRESS BOX INTO THE DRIVER'S BOOT OF THE STAGECOACH.

Minutes later, Jack Almer, who went by the name Jack Averill, bought a ticket to Riverside and boarded the stage. Almer happened to be leader of the Red Jack gang, which raided stagecoaches throughout southeastern Arizona, around the Florence-Globe area. The gang would sweep out of the San Pedro Valley, guns blazing, robbing stagecoaches, and then disappear into the nearby mountains.

On August 10, 1883, Almer's partners, Charley Hensley and Joe Tuttle, waited in the distance, outside Florence, to see if Almer had boarded the stage, a signal that a treasure box was on board. After spotting him, the two men rode to an area where they planned to ambush the stage. Almer, meanwhile, got off the stage at Riverside, complained angrily when he learned no one left him a horse, and was last seen walking away from the stagecoach stop.

Another version of the story, however, tells of Almer disguised as a woman passenger. According to this particular account, when the Wells Fargo guard denied the stage was carrying any gold, the "female" passenger leaped from the stage calling him a liar. Almer, dressed as a woman, supposedly shot the guard when he went for his gun. Although the story gets a lot of play, its veracity is doubtful, especially since someone else was identified as the only passenger in the coach when it left Riverside.

Veteran stagecoach whip Watson Humphreys handled the reins that day. Along side him sat 23-year Johnny Collins, a Wells Fargo & Company shotgun messenger. The lone passenger was Felix LeBlanc of Evans & LeBlance merchants of Riverside. Two miles out of Riverside, not far from the mining town of Pioneer, the coach slowed as it approached an upgrade, and—without warning—gunshots filled the air, catching the stage in crossfire. Tuttle opened fire with a shotgun striking Collins in the neck and chin. Hensley squeezed off seven successive shots with his Winchester. Bullets slammed into Collins' neck killing him instantly. One of the shots killed one of the lead horses and wounded another. Another bullet grazed Humphrey above one of his knees, who raised his hands, and shouted.

"For God's sake, stop shooing, you have killed one man, what more do you want!"

The bandits, faces hidden by red calico hoods, emerged from hiding and ordered LeBlanc out of the passenger compartment, took the money he carried, and then told him to help Humphreys to lower the strongbox. The highwaymen handed LeBlanc a hatchet and told him to break open the box. Inside were two bags of silver coin, weighing sixty pounds apiece. They were valued at about $2,000, along with $620 in gold coins. The two men transferred the loot onto one of the stagecoach horses and left.

A manhunt was quickly organized. Wanted posters were printed and posted with Wells Fargo, Arizona Territory, and Pinal County authorities offered rewards of $1,500 for each of the killers. A posse, headed by Sheriff Bob Paul, eventually tracked down every member of the gang. On the night of October 4, 1883, Hensley and Red Jack Almer were killed in a fierce gun battle with Paul and his men. The silver and gold coins taken in the robbery were never recovered. Much of the money taken in the gang's stagecoach robberies, around $8,000, was supposedly buried around its hideout in the Wilcox area.

Historians say at least 134 stagecoaches were robbed in Arizona between 1875 and 1903. Half of the holdups were never solved. Officials say eighty outlaws were caught and sent to prison. Several more were hanged. And a few were killed trying to flee from the law.

THIRTY-FOUR

TO LIVE & DIE
BY THE GUN

THE EX-LAWMAN STOOD OUTSIDE THE WHITE ELEPHANT SALOON AND GAMBLING HOUSE IN FORT WORTH, TEXAS, ON THE NIGHT OF FEBRUARY 8, 1887, GLANCED AT HIS POCKET WATCH AND, IN A LOUD VOICE, CALLED FOR LUKE SHORT TO JOIN HIM.

Short, a gunfighter, gambler, and bar owner who managed the White Elephant, came outside about 8 p.m. Staying parallel of each other, the two men inched their way up the street about a block and stopped in front of the Shooting Gallery, a bar and brothel. The other man was Tim Isaiah Courtright, born in Sangamon County, Illinois, in the spring of 1845 or 1848. He spent most of his adult life living by the gun, including service as an infantryman in the Civil War under General John Logan. Courtright even won praise for his bravery.

After the war, he worked for Logan as an Army scout, tagged with the nickname, Longhair, because he wore his hair in the style of other scouts. Courtright was also mistakenly referred to as Jim, although the name stuck. Courtright, who wore twin six-shooters, butts forward, earned the reputation as a fast gun, supposedly faster than other well-known gunmen of the time.

In 1870, he married Sarah Elizabeth Weeks. Three years later, they moved to an area around Fort Worth, Texas, area and tried to make a go of it farming, but failed. When the couple moved to town, Courtright worked at various jobs, including that of a city jailer, deputy sheriff, deputy US Marshal, a private detective, and a hired killer for his former Army commander, Black Jack Logan, who owned a ranch in New Mexico. He ran for city marshal in 1876, won by three votes, and assumed responsibility for keeping the peace in Fort Worth's Hells Half Acre, the town's red-light district.

Courtright found himself in a number of confrontations and gunned down several men in his role of lawman. As city marshal, he incurred the wrath of city officials and merchants because he tried to clean up the vice and crime rampant in Fort Worth. He was told to limit his job as city marshal to simply "keep the peace"— nothing more. The red light district provided an income stream that merchants didn't want to see ended. In 1879, he ran for a fourth term but lost.

Courtright, already known as a fearless gunman, had an even darker side. He operated a protection racket, and pressured business owners in the Hells Half Acre district to pay for the service or risk make an enemy of Courtright. It's believed, although specifics aren't clear, that Luke Short refused Courtright's attempt at extortion. Some accounts say the two men clashed over an attempt to gain control of the gambling interests in Fort Worth. Although friends at one time, the relationship had soured to a mutual dislike and, according to some historians, Courtright decided to make an example of Short.

Facing each other in front of the *Shooting Gallery*, the two men exchanged a few bitter words. Courtright, who had been drinking, made some comment about Short having a gun. But Short denied it and even opened his vest to show Courtright he had no gun.

"Don't you pull a gun on me," Courtright said in a loud voice, and drew a pistol from his right hip with his right hand. Somehow, the gun got tangled in his watch-chain—just enough of a delay to allow Short to pull his own gun and fire. The bullet ripped off Courtright's thumb on his shooting hand. As he tried to shift the gun to his other hand, Short squeezed off four more shots, all of which hit the gunman. Bleeding and in shock, Longhair Jim Courtright fell backwards into the street, and died a short while later. Short went on trial for the shooting, but was exonerated after it was ruled justified self-defense.

THIRTY-FIVE

LEGACY OF MURDER
& MAYHEM

A SMALL BAND OF MOSTLY OLD MEN, WOMEN, AND CHILDREN, INTENT ON LEAVING ARKANSAS, WAS HEADED FURTHER WEST IN NOVEMBER 1864, FOR WHAT THEY HOPED WAS A BETTER LIFE, AWAY FROM TURMOIL OF THE CIVIL WAR.

Unknown to them, the settlers were being watched by desperado Cullen Montgomery Baker and his so-called Rangers, or Jayhawkers. Baker considered it unpatriotic for anyone to flee the state. The Rangers caught up to the group just as they were crossing the Saline River, somewhere in the Ouachita Mountains. The confrontation triggered an argument, but the settlers refused to back down or turn around. That's when Baker slipped his pistol from the holster, and shot and killed the group's leader. Baker assured the rest of the group, now distraught and in shock, that if they returned to his side of the river, no one else would be hurt. Moments later, when the settlers reached the other side, Baker and his men shot and killed nine other men, an event known as the Massacre of Saline.

Mean and cold-blooded were the best words to describe Baker. Considered one of the most ruthless killers who ever lived, he left a trail of bodies—men and women—across the American frontier. Baker, one of seven children, was born June 22, 1835, in Weakley County, Tennessee. A few years later, his family moved to Texas. Trouble, and emotional issues, seemed to be Baker's constant companion from early in life. He left home in 1854 and drifted across Texas and Oklahoma, before finding his way into Arkansas and Kansas territories a couple of years later.

He also got married in 1854, but settling down did little to quell his thirst for drinking and fighting. The booze, some historians contend, fueled a vicious temper. In 1857, Mary Jane (Petty) Baker gave birth to a baby girl, but died three years later. Baker took his daughter back to Texas to leave her with his in-laws.

Baker joined the Confederacy during the Civil War and served as a member of Morgan's Squadron, a Confederate cavalry unit. But, he deserted. Later, he served with the 15th Texas Cavalry, but was discharged because of a disability. One writer described Baker's time as a soldier:

> "Insubordinate by nature and a coward at heart, there was poorer soldier in the ranks on either side than this shirking ruffian, and his desertion in a few weeks was not looked upon as a loss by other men or officers."

Not only was Baker a coward and back-shooter, he killed with little motive. One report tells of the time he was on his way home from the army and came upon a group of immigrants in Sevier County, Tennessee. He spotted a black woman on one of the wagons, apparently expressed his dislike for her and, without provocation, shot and killed her. Baker despised the idea of Reconstruction and, following the Civil War, initiated a one-man war against it around

Texas and Arkansas. Along the way, he established a reputation for violence. In fact, it's said that most of the people he killed after the war were former slaves along with whites whom he considered carpetbaggers, and Union sympathizers. He and his outlaw gang swept across the territory robbing and killing, and managed to elude Union troops dispatched to put an end to his reign of terror.

Baker remarried in 1862 and moved to Cass County, Texas, where he tried to make a living operating a ferry business. His wife, Martha, died four years later. Her passing plunged him into a deep state of depression. Despite his mental state, Baker proposed to Martha's sister, Belle, a couple of months later, but she rejected the proposal and married Thomas Orr, a schoolteacher and political activist. The two men had clashed in the past. Baker, according to one account, tried to hang Orr from the limb of a tree. Orr presumably pretended to be dead and was mistakenly cut down too soon.

The gunman eventually ended up in Boot Hill along with other frontier killers, but there are several versions of his demise on January 6, 1869. According to one story, Baker was poisoned by a dose of strychnine by his wife's family, and then shot to death. Another version says he was killed at the home of his former father-in-law by a group of men from the community.

The third account points to Orr and three other men who reportedly followed Baker and an accomplice to what they believed was a hideout in southeastern Arkansas, charged in with guns blazing, and killed the two of them where they stood. Regardless of the method, Cullen Montgomery Baker, the most-feared gunman in the Lone Star State, was dead at 34.

THIRTY-SIX

HANGING OF AN INNOCENT MAN

O N THE NIGHT OF MARCH 28, 1881, MILT YARBERRY, WALKED ALONG A STREET IN ALBUQUERQUE, NEW MEXICO, HOLDING THE HAND OF THE FIVE-YEAR OLD DAUGHTER OF THE WOMAN HE LIVED WITH, AND TOOK HER INTO GERARD'S RESTAURANT TO LEAVE HER WITH SADIE PRESTON, THE MOTHER.

Just minutes before, Preston was sitting with self-proclaimed gunman Harry A. Brown, with whom she was having an affair. Yarberry, the first town marshal of Albuquerque, then left the restaurant and confronted Brown, who had ducked outside when he was told the marshal was on his way. A witness said the two men exchanged bitter words and moved to a nearby vacant lot. Brown often bragged to anyone who would listen about how many men he had gunned down, even though no one ever heard of him shooting anyone.

He quickly got the reputation of a heavy drinker who needed little provocation to draw his gun.

While the two men argued, Sadie Preston stepped out of the restaurant and called for Brown. When Yarberry turned toward her, Brown hit him in the face, drew his gun and fired. The bullet creased Yarberry's hand. The lawman drew his own gun and squeezed off two shots, both hitting Brown in the chest. The man was dead before he hit the ground. Benalilo County Sheriff Perfecto Armijo, who supported Yarberry's appointment as town marshal, had no choice but to arrest Yarberry, who claimed self-defense. He was eventually acquitted.

Before Yarberry took the job in Albuquerque as a lawman, he had been on the run from a life as an outlaw. In fact, author Robert K. DeArment, in his book, Deadly Dozen labeled him one of the twelve least-known but most-dangerous gunmen in the Old West. Born in Walnut Ridge, Arkansas, in 1849, he left home and changed his name from John Armstrong to Milt Yarberry after being accused of killing a man over a land dispute. Wanted for murder, Yarberry killed another man in Helena, Arkansas, in 1873, and went on the run again.

Two years later, he killed again. This time, the victim was a man he suspected of being a bounty hunter trying to collect the $200 reward posted for him. Yarberry, constantly on the run, crossed into Texas and opened a saloon in Decatur with a partner. When a bounty hunter showed up asking questions, he sold out to his partner and left town. The bounty hunter's body was discovered days later outside Decatur. He had been shot to death.

Yarberry ended up in Canon City, Colorado, opened the *Gem*, a saloon and variety hall with Tony Preston. One day, a bartender shot Preston. When he recovered, Yarberry sold out to him and moved on to Las Vegas, New Mexico. While there, he operated a brothel catering to railroad workers. Again, trouble chased him away. This time, he was suspected, but not charged, with killing a man, supposedly over a prostitute. Yarberry eventually ended up in San Mariel, New Mexico, where his former partner Tony Preston was operating a business. Yarberry got involved with Preston's wife. He left town a short time later and took Sadie and her four-year old daughter with him to Albuquerque.

Less than a month after the confrontation where he shot Harry A. Brown, Yarberry shot another man, and got arrested again. After a three-day trial, he was sentenced to hang. On September 8, 1882, he and three others managed to escape from the Santa Fe jail. Four days later, a posse tracked him down and took him into custody. Several appeals were denied. No amount of explaining could delay the inevitable. On February 9, 1883, Yarberry went to the gallows, where Sheriff Armijo, his good friend, was assigned to pull the lever. His last words: "Gentlemen, you are hanging an innocent man."

THIRTY-SEVEN

DARING
& DYNAMITE

THE ENGINEER OF THE WESTBOUND UNION PACIFIC SNAPPED OPEN HIS POCKET WATCH JUST AS THE BIG LOCOMOTIVE REACHED MILEPOST 609, NEAR WILCOX, WYOMING. HE NOTED THE TIME, AND LOOKED UP.

Squinting through a steady drizzle, he spotted two men with lanterns in the distance, flagging him down. Engineer W.R. "Grindstone" Jones, thinking the rain might have washed out a small wooden bridge up ahead, applied the brake and brought the first section of the Union Pacific Overland Flyer No. 1 to a halt about 2:20 am, Friday, June 2, 1899. The train had two sections; each pulled its own locomotive.

As the locomotive rolled to a stop, two armed masked men boarded, and forced Jones and his, fireman, a man named Dietrick, to pull forward across the bridge. As it reached the other side, other gang members ignited dynamite. The explosion prevented the train's second section from following. Jones and Dietrick were then ordered to uncouple the passenger cars, and then pull the engine ahead for another two miles. Waiting were four more outlaws. At gunpoint, Jones and Dietrick were escorted to the mail car.

The outlaws ordered clerks Robert Lawson and Burt Bruce to open the door. When they refused, the robbers dynamited the door open. But, the pickings were slim. The bandits then headed for the express car where Messenger Charles Woodcock also refused to open the door. But, as before, gang members blew the door open. Once inside, they dynamited the safe. The explosion was so fierce it also blew out the sides and roof of the express car.

In the couple of hours, six bandits collected unsigned bank notes, diamonds, and jewelry. Some reports say a lot of money was lost in the explosions. After the gang left and headed for the mountains, Jones and his crew nursed the damaged train for about 12 miles into Medicine Bow where a telegram was sent reporting the holdup. The Union Pacific dispatched the No. 4, a special train in Laramie carrying a posse as well as cars for horses and equipment. It arrived at the scene of the robbery about 9 am. A posse of 100 men was formed and included a detective force from the Union Pacific and Burlington Railroad, along with the Pinkerton Detective Agency, local posses, and Company C of the state militia.

Authorities blamed the robbery on the Wild Bunch, and an $18,000 reward was offered for their capture—dead or alive. The Union Pacific offered a $1,000 reward for each of the six train robbers. The Pacific Express Company, whose safe was robbed, matched the reward offer, as did the US government.

The stolen notes began showing up across the southwest, but by the time lawmen traced them, the robbers were long gone. The initial estimate of the loss was put at $30,000. Several years later, however, railroad authorities put the total loss at $50,000. None of the money was recovered.

THIRTY-EIGHT

FROM OUTLAW TO ACTOR

OUTLAW ROY DOUGHERTY, KEEPING LOW, RAN FROM THE SALOON TO A NEARBY BARN IN INGALLS, OKLAHOMA, POSITIONED HIM-SELF UP HIGH, TOOK AIM AND GUNNED DOWN DEPUTY MARSHAL THOMAS HUESTON, WHO WOULD DIE THE NEXT DAY.

Fourteen US Marshals had closed in on members of the Doolin-Dalton Gang, also known as the Wild Bunch. The furious confron-tation, known as the *Battle of Ingalls*, took place in the afternoon of September 1, 1893. A lot of blood spilled in the battle that claimed the lives of three deputy marshals and a bystander. Bill Doolin and his gang, several wounded, managed to escape with the exception of Dougherty, also known as Arkansas Tom Jones. He stayed hid-den until Deputy Marshal Jim Masterson hurled a stick of dynamite into the barn. The explosion stunned the shooter long enough for him to be taken into custody.

Dougherty was born in Missouri on New Year's Day, 1870. The family was strict in terms of religion and his two brothers became preachers. Dougherty, however, had a rebellious streak and left home at 14 to head for the Oklahoma Territory. Once there he began also using the name *Arkansas Tom Jones*, telling people he was from Arkansas. He worked as a cowboy for several years and, along the way, met Bill Doolin, and joined his gang around 1892, participating in a number of robberies.

For his role in the Battle of Ingalls, Dougherty was sentenced to fifty years behind bars. His two preacher brothers intervened and Dougherty was paroled in 1910. He ran a restaurant for a couple of years in Drumright, Oklahoma, but found the business boring, and took to the road, ending up in Hollywood where he hoped to act in Western films. Dougherty actually got a role in a silent film, in 1915, called *Passing of the Oklahoma Cowboys*. The film, directed by noted Western lawman Bill Tilghman, was aimed at depicting the end of outlaw gangs. Dougherty, the only survivor of the Doolin-Dalton Gang, played himself.

Despite his freedom, Dougherty could not live life on the straight-and-narrow. In 1917, he held up a bank in Neosho, Missouri, and was captured and sent to prison. He was released in 1921, but went back on the outlaw trail. Shortly after being released, he robbed another bank, this one in Asbury, Missouri, and went on the run from the law again. Lawman tracked Dougherty to Joplin, Missouri, where he engaged in a gun battle, and got killed August 16, 1924. He was 54 years old.

THIRTY-NINE

BILL DOOLIN'S LUCKY DAY

ON THE MORNING OF OCTOBER 5, 1892, A GROUP OF SIX MEN GALLOPED TOWARD THE SMALL TOWN OF COFFEYVILLE, KANSAS, TO MAKE OUTLAW HISTORY BY ROBBING TWO BANKS SIMULTA-NEOUSLY, BUT ONE OF THEM SENSED AN IMPENDING DANGER.

Bill Doolin, a member of the Dalton Gang, suddenly pulled back on the reins and slowed his horse to a stop, pretending it had thrown a shoe, and explained he was heading to a nearby ranch to replace it. Doolin wasn't comfortable with the plan from the beginning. Since the Dalton Gang was so successful at robbing trains full-time, he didn't think the sudden switch to bank robbery was a good idea. The Daltons had moved to Coffeyville in 1886, and lived there for a short time. For this reason, Doolin found it amusing that gang members disguised themselves with false beards and wigs. He knew the disguises wouldn't fool anyone.

Gang leader Bob Dalton committed himself to carrying out the raid, declaring he wanted to be remembered for doing something Jesse James never did: "rob two banks at once in broad daylight." The robbery attempt ended in total disaster when the citizens of Coffeyville turned the tables and killed everyone in the gang but Emmett Dalton.

According to another account, Doolin did head into Coffeyville after all, but hightailed it when he saw his associates dead in the street. Yet another story suggests that Doolin and Bob Dalton parted ways before the robbery attempt after quibbling over how the money would be split. Regardless of what actually happened, one fact was clear: Bill Doolin was alive. Bob Dalton was dead. Doolin then formed his own gang, which became known as another faction of the *Wild Bunch*. During the 1890s, the gang became known as one of the most powerful in the southwest, terrorizing banks, trains, and stagecoaches throughout Arkansas, southern Kansas, and the Indian Territory. Over a four-year period, Doolin's outlaws amassed an estimated $165,000 in stolen loot.

William Doolin, born in 1858 on a homestead near Big Piney River in Johnson County, Arkansas, left home at 23 to work as a cowboy in Indian Territory, which became Oklahoma Territory in 1890. Doolin's marauding ways drew the full attention of E.D. Nix, a Guthrie, Oklahoma, businessman who was appointed US Marshal on July 1, 1893. Nix wasted no time in putting together a posse of over a hundred field deputies, including Heck Thomas, Chris Madsen, and Bill Tilghman, known as the *Three Guardsmen*. In late August, Nix sent a posse of thirteen to Ingalls, Oklahoma, to confront Doolin and is gang. In what many historical accounts rank as the deadliest *gun battle* between outlaws and US Marshals in the history of the southwest, six posse members were wounded or killed, but Doolin and others got away.

After Tilghman won appointment as US Marshal, he tracked Doolin to Eureka Springs where the outlaw went to recuperate from gunshot wounds. The lawman managed to take Doolin into custody on January 15, 1896. He was indicted in Stillwater, Oklahoma, in connection for the shooting in Ingalls, but entered a plea of not guilty. Right before his trial, on the night of July 5, Doolin and several other inmates escaped from the Guthrie Federal Prison.

Marshal Heck Thomas, a Tilghman associate, learned he was hiding in a barn at the home of his father-in-law and, with a posse, tracked him down. Doolin came out of barn firing, but Thomas and his nine deputies fired back, killing him. Historians say nearly every member of Doolin's outfit met violent deaths.

FORTY

A SADISTIC BULLY

Deputy US Marshal Bob Olinger and a horse thief by the name of Pas Chavez walked toward each other along the main street of Seven Rivers, New Mexico, in mid-1878. A few days before, the two men had exchanged bitter words during a card game at the Royal Saloon.

Olinger, a big, broad-shouldered man of six-feet and about 240 pounds, extended his hand as they neared each other. When Chavez grabbed it, Olinger jerked him off balance, jammed a revolver into Chavez' stomach and fired. According to one account, Chavez fell dead in the street. But, he may have survived the wound because another report had him being hanged for theft in Lincoln County two years later.

Charles Robert "Bob" Olinger was born in 1841, either in Ohio or Indiana. In 1876, he joined his brother John Wallace Olinger in Seven Rivers where both became members of the Seven Rivers Warriors, a gang of rustlers. Both brothers battled on the

Murphy-Dolan-Riley side in the *Lincoln County War.* This association brought Olinger into a parallel confrontation with Billy the Kid, who had killed Olinger's close friend, Bob Beckwith, during the Lincoln County battle.

Most folks who knew Olinger considered him a bully with a reputation for being sadistic and dangerous because of his quick gun and hair-trigger temper. Even though he served as a deputy US marshal, historian Jay Robert Nash wrote that Olinger was "better suited to fighting range wars than upholding the peace."

In November 1880, Pat Garrett, who pledged to rid the Lincoln County area of rustlers, was elected sheriff. The next month, he assembled a posse to pursue Billy the Kid and captured him just before the end of the year. The following April, the young outlaw was tried and convicted of murdering Lincoln County Sheriff William Brady and sentenced to hang—the only conviction ever obtained against those involved in the Lincoln County War. The Kid was transported to Lincoln where he was placed under 24-hour guard on the top floor of the town courthouse by two of Garrett's deputies, James Bell and Olinger. Garrett warned the two men to stay vigilant and watch their prisoner every moment of his captivity because, if given a change, Billy the Kid would try to escape and kill them in the process.

Olinger told Garrett the Kid had no chance of escaping. He took every opportunity to bully Billy, constantly terrorizing him by beating him or insulting him. He often threatened the Kid with a ten-gauge double-barreled shotgun. Billy told a friend that Olinger's abuse "used to work me up until I could hardly contain myself."

On April 28, 1881, with Garrett away on business, Olinger left the courthouse to escort several other prisoners to a meal at the Wortley Hotel. He left his shotgun behind with Bell, who had established an amicable relationship with Billy. Confined by leg irons and handcuffs, the Kid asked Bell to escort him to the outhouse at the back of the courthouse. When they returned, Billy made his move to escape. Although the details are unclear, the Kid was somehow able to get hold of a gun and kill Bell.

Olinger heard the blast, and hurried back to the courthouse. Billy, meanwhile, retrieved Olinger's shotgun and took up a position at a window overlooking the courtyard. When Olinger came into view, Billy aimed the deputy's own shotgun, called out, "Hello, Bob," and fired both barrels, killing him. According to one account Billy smashed Olinger's shotgun against a porch railing and threw the pieces at the deputy's corpse.

Olinger, who was gunned down at 40, is buried in an unmarked grave at Fort Stanton Cemetery in Lincoln County.

FORTY-ONE

BOLD & SHAMELESS TERROR

ON A MOONLIT NIGHT IN JUNE 1873, BILL POSEY AND HIS GANG FORCED THEIR WAY INTO THE HOME OF MATT AND SARAH WALLACE OUTSIDE WACO, TEXAS, AND DRAGGED THE HUSBAND OUTSIDE. SARAH, HOLDING THEIR BEWILDERED TWO-YEAR OLD DAUGHTER, SCREAMED IN PROTEST, BUT HER PLEAS WERE IGNORED.

Sarah Wallace, powerless to intervene, watched as her husband's hands were tied behind his back and he was lifted onto a horse. One gang member threw a rope with a hangman's noose over a branch of a Live oak tree, and another tightened it around the man's neck. Seconds later, someone slapped the rump of the horse. The rope snapped Wallace's neck, leaving his lifeless body swaying and turning in the still of the night. The only sounds were the creaking of the rope against the limb and the weeping of mother and daughter as they stared in horror. Sarah Wallace was six-months pregnant with their second child.

The leader of the gang that lynched Wallace was Bill Posey—the dead man's own brother-in-law. Born June 16, 1846, in Talapoosa, Alabama, William Andrew Jackson Posey was the fourteenth of fifteen children. His parents, Benjamin Franklin Posey and Eliza Berryhill, were first cousins and each was one-half Creek Indian, as were their children. Not long after he was born, the family moved to Nacogdoches County, Texas.

Posey served with the Confederacy in the Civil War, but deserted at Camp Hood on Padre Island in 1864. The following year, he married Elizabeth Wallace. The couple settled on Tehuacana Creek, north of Waco, near Matt and Sarah Wallace. The two couples went into business together driving cattle along the Chisholm Trail to Kansas to take advantage of the East's hunger for beef.

At the time, cattle was three-dollars a head in Texas, but worth $15 a head at railheads in Kansas. Posey used the profits to buy land around Waco, including 500 acres along the Brazos River, just east of town. He also bought the 666 acres of land inherited by Sarah Miller Wallace for $5,000, payable at $1,000 for five years. During the acquisition of these stretches of land, accusations of cattle rustling started to emerge. Livestock displaying the brands of other ranches were spotted in Posey's herds, prompting charges of theft to be filed against him. The allegations persuaded the Wallaces to distance themselves from any further business dealings with Posey.

Although not a lot of information about Posey exists, what little that is known points to him as a bold and shameless cowboy who terrorized Texas and the Indian Territory. Posey and his men rustled herds of cattle, waged mayhem in towns during violent drinking binges, tormenting citizens and defying the law. Sometimes, their indiscriminate shooting left innocent victims wounded.

When a deputy sheriff tried to intervene in one of the towns, Posey reportedly killed him in a saloon shootout on the Guadalupe, and then scalped him. In the summer of 1874, Posey was arrested and convicted for stealing mules and sentenced to a five-year prison term. Prisoner #3644 was put behind bars on July 11, 1874, but escaped less than two years later, and fled into Indian Territory. Along the way, he stopped to threaten the lives of prosecutors and attorneys who helped convict him.

From Indian Territory, Posey and his men resumed cattle rustling raids into Texas. On April 6, 1877, the gang took forty head of cattle from a rancher named Charles Clinton. At Fort Smith, Judge Isaac Parker issued an arrest warrant and dispatched deputies to take him in. According to newspaper report from Fort Smith, Posey agreed to return with the deputies but, first, invited them in for a meal. While they were eating, he retrieved a hidden gun and started shooting, hitting a deputy in the eye, another in the leg. He shredded the warrant, and warned the lawmen the same fate awaited anyone else who tried to take him in.

Posey's reign of terror ended when he was killed in 1877 in a bloody shootout in Indian Territory with the Creek Nation Lighthorse Police. He was only 31, a man without a moral compass who thought nothing of killing even his own family members.

FORTY-TWO

JESSE JAMES LAST ROBBERY

T HE THREE MEN SAT ON HORSEBACK WAITING IN A GROVE OF CYPRUS TREES, SOAKED TO THE SKIN, HATS PULLED LOW AND HUNCHED OVER, TRYING TO SHIELD THEMSELVES FROM A RELENTLESS RAINFALL.

In the midst of a howling wind, they detected hoof beats and spotted paymaster Alexander Smith approaching the gate between Shoal Creek and the US Army Corps of Engineers' Blue Water Camp in Alabama. As he leaned over to open it, Jesse James, William "Whiskey Head" Ryan, and Wood Hite, thundered from their hiding place and surrounded him, guns drawn. Smith had just returned from Florence, Alabama, carrying a payroll of $5,240.18, to pay laborers working at the Muscle Shoals Canal Project on the Tennessee River.

Jesse James didn't realize it at the time, but this robbery—Friday, March 11, 1881—would be the last of his lengthy and infamous career. Whiskey Head Ryan found the payroll in an inner pocket of Smith's coat, along with a gold watch and about $200 in personal cash. In the meantime, Hite, who happened to be Jesse James' cousin, untied a bag dangling from the pommel of Smith's saddle and discovered it filled with gold and silver coins.

When the outlaws left, they took Smith with them, pushing their horses through a driving rainstorm for about twenty miles, and then pulled up. They returned the gold watch to Smith, gave him back the cash that belonged to him, let him keep his horse, and sent him on his way. Smith didn't get back until the next morning. A posse was quickly assembled and pursued the gang to the north. The trail turned cold when they reached the Cumberland River. The heavy rain had washed away the tracks they were following.

The outlaw trio rode for Nashville, but split up with James headed to his home where he met up with Frank and told him about the robbery. Although Frank James was part of the gang that disbanded a couple of years previous, he had decided to step away from a life of crime and settle down. With most of the original gang either dead or in jail, Jesse formed a new one in 1879, and robbed three trains before the robbery at Blue Water Camp.

About two weeks after the robbery, Whiskey Head Ryan wandered into a saloon at the western edge of Nashville and eventually drank his way into a drunken brawl and got arrested. When lawmen found a quantity of gold on him, they put two-and-two together and arrested him for his role in the robbery of the paymaster. When the James brothers got word of the arrest, they packed up their families and headed out of Nashville. Frank went to Virginia, while Jesse traveled to St. Joseph, Missouri, and took the name Thomas Howard and began forming another gang.

A few months later, in the spring of 1882, gang member Robert Ford shot James in the back of the head in his St. Joseph home and he died on the spot. Six months later, Frank James turned himself in and went on trial for the payroll robbery, but was acquitted. He lived out his life in peace until his death in 1915. Ryan, meanwhile, had been arrested for robbing a train in Missouri and sentenced to 25 years, but got an early release in 1889. He died a short time later when he hit his head on a tree branch while riding his horse at full gallop. Wood Hite, the third man involved in the Blue Water Camp robbery, had been shot to death in December 1881. The shooter was Robert Ford who, a year later, would kill Jesse James.

FORTY-THREE

A DEADLY GUNSLINGER

THE HANGMAN SLIPPED THE BLACK CAP OVER THE PRISONER'S FACE, ADJUSTED THE ROPE AROUND HIS NECK, AND SAID, "ALL READY." AT 2:37 ON OCTOBER 11, 1878, THE TRAP DOOR OF THE GALLOWS GAVE WAY AND THE DOOMED MAN FELL EIGHT FEET TO WHAT WAS SUPPOSED TO BE HIS DEATH.

The hangman had allowed too much slack and the prisoner hit the ground with both feet, still living and still breathing. As the crowd of more than four thousand fell silent, the rope was re-adjusted, and he was lifted up so he could hang again. After dangling for a little over eleven minutes, Wild Bill Longley choked to death. Longley wore a reputation as one of the most ruthless killers on the frontier. At 16 years of age, he weighed 200 pounds distributed around a six-foot frame that rippled with muscles, proportioned in a way that made him appear slender. His narrow eyes, the window to a man's soul, were dark, cold, brooding, and veiled a quick-tempered evil rarely seen in someone so young.

Born Oct. 6, 1851, in a small farming community in Mill Creek, Texas, the family moved a few years later to Evergreen, where Longley carried out chores on the family farm. He taught himself to use a gun, which he carried to hunt for food in the woods. When he reached his teens, Texas and other southern states were emerging from the Civil War under Reconstruction, during which Longley developed a deep, simmering hatred of Northerners and ex-slaves.

On a December day in 1866, he and his father were strolling through Evergreen when a relatively new deputized former slave, drunk and disorderly, hurled an insult at Campbell Longley. Without a thought or hesitation, Wild Bill ripped his revolver from its holster and killed the man in less than a few seconds. Longley hadn't yet reached 16. Forced to flee, he joined a small gang that spent its time terrorizing and killing former slaves along with anyone they considered Yankee sympathizers.

Longley never killed anyone for financial gain. The shootings almost always revolved around wanting to teach the other person a lesson, or righting what he considered were personal wrongs. The killing, mostly racial, continued, year-after-year. He gunned down men and women. Gender didn't matter. He was arrested several times, but always managed to escape. In a three-year span, 1873 to 1876, Longley killed four more men before heading for Louisiana. But it was there he was captured and returned to Texas to stand trial for one of the murders he previously committed.

The jury deliberated less than two hours before sentencing him to hang. In his cell, Longley began writing letters. Some were sent to newspapers, detailing his life story. He also wrote the governor seeking clemency. He pointed out to the governor than John Wesley Hardin got only 25 years for killing 40 people and wanted to know why he was being sent to the gallows for killing 32. The governor never bothered to respond.

Before Longley's walk up the steps to the gallows, he repented. In Giddings, he told the assembled crowd he had really only killed eight men—not the 32 he bragged about, as though the revised number would help in his salvation.

"I deserved this fate," he said in a final goodbye. "It is a debt I have owed for a wild and reckless life...so long, everybody!"

FORTY-FOUR

A VIGILANTE CALLED "X"

TWO WAGONS SERVED AS THE JUDGE'S BENCH AND WITNESS BOX FOR THE THREE-DAY OUTDOOR TRIAL OF GEORGE IVES AT NEVADA CITY, MONTANA, IN DECEMBER 1863, CONVICTED OF ROBBING AND RUTHLESS KILLING OF YOUNG NICHOLAS TBALT, A POPULAR LOCAL MAN NICKNAMED *DUTCHMAN*.

The jury returned the verdict in less than an hour, directing Ives to be hanged immediately from the rafter of an unfinished building. Everyone seemed to fear Ives, even his own associates. Tall, cool-headed, and fearless, he was responsible for a number of crimes that involved robbery and murder. But, on this day, he delivered an unsuccessful plea seeking a stay of execution until the following morning.

"Ask him how much time he gave the Dutchman," roared John X. Beidler, a member of the Vigilante Committee that executed Ives a few hours later.

The death of Tbalt, believed to be in his teens, so incensed the community that a group of residents, tired of marauding bandits and ineffective law enforcement, agreed to band together to bring Ives to justice. At the time, Montana wasn't a state or even a territory, so no official law existed. And, population was on the upswing.

By fall 1863, about 10,000 residents moved into Alder Gulch and other towns along a 14-mile stretch, including Nevada City and Virginia City. Members of the highly-secretive Vigilante Committee consisted of men from Nevada City and adjoining Virginia City, and from Bannock, about 75 miles away. Their purpose: To systematically track down and hang lawbreakers, including Sheriff Henry Plummer who, they believed, served as leader of the road agents.

Beidler, who preferred to be known only as "X," became one of the most active members but, unlike the others, he didn't bother to hide his identify. In fact, he apparently liked the recognition. Born in Pennsylvania, Beidler worked as a shoemaker and brick maker before he left for Kansas to try his hand at farming. He was a fierce supporter of John Brown's radical abolitionist movement. But, when *Brown* was captured and executed for his failed raid on Harper's Ferry armory in Virginia, Beidler traveled to Texas. From Texas, he headed north to join the gold rush in Montana, part of the newly-formed Idaho Territory, in March 1863. The promise of wealth attracted hordes of settlers and by July of the following year, the population in the Alder Gulch area would swell to more than 30,000.

Beidler was a small man - about five-and-a-half feet tall - but deadly with firearms. Some accounts say he also managed to intimidate others because he was "mean and nasty and knew he could outdraw them." Historian Jon Axline, in his book *Still Speaking Ill of the Dead,* wrote that most of the outlaws Beidler hunted down as a member of the Vigilante Committee, weren't brought back for trial; they were either shot or hanged. In fact, Beidler personally handled the hanging of five Plummer gang members on January 14, 1864.

When the Vigilante Committee disbanded, he went to work as a stagecoach guard. He was also appointed a U.S. Deputy Marshal. When he returned east in 1888 for a visit, he was flat broke. "I made fortunes for others, but none for myself," he once told a friend. The Montana Territorial Legislature considered a bill aimed at providing Beidler with financial support, but it was soundly defeated.

Axline said, in his 2005 book, that "X" spent his final years living "largely on the charity of friends." He also earned a little income by telling stories at local bars and restaurants around Helena. John X. Beidler died on January 22, 1890, at the Pacific Hotel in Helena from complications due to pneumonia. His death certificate listed his occupation as *Public Benefactor.* The Society of Montana Pioneers erected a plague in his honor, hailing him as a *Brave Pioneer.*

FORTY-FIVE

RIDING WITH THE WILD BUNCH

O N A CHILLY DAY IN JANUARY 1906, PRISONER 1348 WALKED OUT OF THE WHITEWASHED WALLS OF NEW MEXICO TERRITORIAL PRISON TO HIS FREEDOM AFTER ONCE BEING SENTENCED TO LIFE IMPRISONMENT.

William Ellsworth Lay—also known as *Elzy* or *Elza,* and by the alias, *William McGinnis*—rode with the Wild Bunch in the 1890s, a close ally of Butch Cassidy. Elzy was born November 25, 1862, in Adams County, Ohio. It's believed he traveled to the Denver area looking for work, and was hired on at the Bassett ranch in Brown's Park, where he met Cassidy. The two were about the same age and discovered a few things in common, including horsemanship skills. Before long, Lay turned outlaw and got involved in cattle rustling, gambling, stealing horses, and even counterfeiting.

When Cassidy formed the Wild Bunch, he invited Lay along. The gang operated out of Hole-in-the-Wall, a hideout situated in a remote area of Wyoming's Big Horn Mountains, one of several hideouts the gang used on a north-south line, about 200 miles long. Cassidy served as leader of nine other outlaws, including Lay who also helped plan the group's robberies. The Wild Bunch achieved a reputation as the most successful train-robbing gang in history.

When the Wild Bunch broke up, Lay hooked up with the Black Jack Ketchum gang. And, that's when life took a turn for the worse. An attempted train robbery, on July 11, 1899, near Folsom, New Mexico, got botched and members of the Ketchum Gang ended up in a shoot-out with the law. During the gun battle, Lay reportedly killed two sheriffs, and was wounded trying to escape. On October 10, 1899, Lay was sentenced to serve the remainder of his life behind bars, under his alias, William McGinnis, at the New Mexico Territorial Prison. *McGinnis* won his freedom for helping put an end to a prison riot. During the riot, several inmates had kidnapped the warden's family, but he intervened, and convinced the prisoners to release the wife and daughter. In return for his courage, Governor Miguel Antonio Otero issued him a pardon.

After being released, Lay made his way to Wyoming where he worked as a bartender, and tried his hand at oil drilling, becoming an amateur geologist. He married and eventually traveled to California where he worked for the Imperial Valley Irrigation System. Lay spent the rest of his life as a respected businessman, and died in Los Angeles on November 10, 1934, an admirable turnaround for a man who expected to live out his years in a cell.

FORTY-SIX

NIGHT OF THE AMBUSH

ON THE NIGHT OF MAY 2, 1895, GEORGE "BITTERCREEK" NEWCOMB AND CHARLEY PIERCE, MEMBERS OF THE WILD BUNCH, RODE INTO THE DUNN RANCH ON THE CIMARRON RIVER NEAR PAWNEE, OKLAHOMA. THEY GUIDED THEIR HORSES INTO THE BARN TO STABLE THEM, UNAWARE OF THE AWAITING DANGER.

Newcomb planned on visiting Rose Dunn, whom he had become romantically involved. She was the teen-age sister of the Dunn brothers, who had introduced the two. But love wasn't in the air on this particular Thursday night. Newcomb and Pierce happened to be on the run with rewards of $5,000 posted for each of them. When the two outlaws left the barn and headed for the ranch boarding house, two shotguns exploded in the black night, cutting them both down. No lawmen were involved in the ambush.

The gunmen were none other than the Dunn Brothers— Bee, Calvin, Dal, George, and Bill.

In addition to operating the boarding house, and a local meat market, the Dunns were involved in other ventures, not all legal. The reward money, obviously, was too good to pass up, which led to the ambush. It's not certain whether Rose had anything to do with the incident. The next day, the part-time bounty hunters loaded the bodies of Newcomb and Pierce into a wagon, took them to Guthrie, and turned them over to authorities to claim the rewards, no questions asked.

Many of the citizens of Pawnee weren't all that fond of the Dunn Brothers. Rumors persisted they were the ones behind a string of cattle rustling incidents, as well as robberies, and some killings. Some accounts say they disposed of the stolen cattle through a Pawnee butcher by the name of G.C. Bolton. The complaints were so extensive that Deputy US Marshal Frank Canton decided to investigate. Canton, incidentally, had once arrested Bill Dunn for rustling, so there was already bad blood between them.

Bill Dunn decided to confront the issue, and rode into Pawnee with one thought in mind: Kill Frank Canton. The sheriff, however, was an established gunman himself, with a reputation for coolness and for being a crack shot. On November 6, 1896, Frank Canton left a restaurant where he served a few court papers, and started walking along the sidewalk. Dunn stepped into the street and fired twice with his revolver, but the bullets missed. Canton pulled his revolver, and quickly returned fire, killing Dunn. The courts ruled the shooting self-defense. Because of their brothers' death, the reputation of the Dunn Brothers suffered a rapid deterioration.

FORTY-SEVEN

AMERICA'S MOST PROLIFIC BANK ROBBER

U S DEPUTY MARSHAL FLOYD WILSON SPOTTED THE MAN HE WAS PURSUING NEAR WOLF CREEK IN OKLAHOMA TERRITORY, AND DROPPED FROM THE SADDLE, RIFLE IN HAND.

"Hold up," he yelled to outlaw Henry Starr, firing a warning shot into the air, "I have a warrant for you." Starr responded by returning fire, wounding Wilson who fell to the ground. Wilson managed to raise the rifle, but it jammed. He reached for his pistol, but it was too late. Starr fired twice more, hitting the marshal again. The young outlaw approached Wilson, stood over him with his Winchester, shot him at point-blank range and escaped on the lawman's horse.

Express company detective H.E. Dickey, who had been delayed in joining Wilson in the chase, witnessed the shootout and cold-blooded killing. Starr would elude Dickey and other lawmen for another seven months until his arrest in Colorado Springs in July 1893. He was extradited to Fort Smith, Arkansas, to stand trial for killing Wilson.

Henry Starr, born December 1873, near Fort Gibson in Indian Territory, now a part of Oklahoma, came from a long line of family criminals. Tom Starr, his grandfather, was also a well-known outlaw. Henry Starr was also the nephew of famed outlaws Sam and Belle Starr. His father and Sam, Belle's husband, were brothers. It's doubtful Henry even knew Belle, since she was killed while he was still in his teens.

By the time he was 20, Starr was already in a gang and well on his way to a life of crime, stealing horses, robbing trains and holding up banks and stagecoaches. During his years on the outlaw trail, Starr killed only one man—Marshal Wilson—which he claimed was done in self-defense.

Judge Isaac Parker didn't buy Starr's argument that Wilson shot at him without provocation, and sentenced Starr to hang on February 20, 1894. But, appeals to the US Supreme Court caused postponements. Parker sentenced him again, but Starr managed to escape the noose on technicalities. The murder conviction was eventually set aside and Starr was sentenced to 15 years for manslaughter and sent to the Ohio Penitentiary, a federal facility, at Columbus. President Theodore Roosevelt commuted the sentence and Starr was released in January 1903. He returned to Tulsa and, several months later, married for the second time.

Starr tried living the honest life, but when he learned officials in Arkansas were seeking his extradition for an 1893 robbery, he went on the run. After teaming up with former partners, Starr's gang resumed its bank robbing ways in 1908, hitting banks in Kansas and Colorado. The law caught up with him again and he was sentenced from seven- to 25-years in the Canon City, Colorado, prison. While there, he wrote his memoirs and eventually was paroled on September 24, 1913. But he still wasn't finished with his outlaw ways.

Between September 8, 1914, and January 13, 1915, Starr was accused of robbing fourteen different banks throughout Oklahoma. Despite the bank-robbing spree, Starr found time for a little self-promotion. During one of his prison stays, he wrote his autobiography, *Thrilling Events: Life of Henry Starr.* In 1919, he got to portray himself in a silent movie, *A Debtor to the Law.* Reform, however, wasn't in the cards for Henry Starr, and he found it impossible to step away from his long life of crime. With one foot in the 19th century and the other in the 20th, Starr failed to recognize the closing of an era.

Starr, who once claimed he robbed more banks than the James-Younger and Doolin-Dalton gangs combined, decided he had one last score in him. On February 18, 1921, Henry and three gang members got in their touring car and drove through the sleet and rain to the People's Bank of Harrison, Arkansas. They entered the bank to rob it of $6,000. But, Bank Manager William J. Myers had other ideas. Grabbing a .38-caliber Winchester from inside the vault, he fired and Starr dropped to the floor, while his partners escaped.

A few days later, 47-year old Henry Starr died with his wife, Hulda, his mother, and his 17-year old son at his side. Starr began his 32 years of crime in 1893 robbing from horseback. It ended when he traveled to his last robbery in a car—making him the first outlaw to use an automobile in a bank robbery.

FORTY-EIGHT

THE BILLY
THE KID WHO WASN'T

AT ABOUT THREE IN THE AFTERNOON ON WEDNESDAY, OCTOBER 26, 1881, BILLY CLAIBORNE MADE HIS WAY ALONG A NARROW LOT A FEW DOORS FROM THE REAR ENTRANCE TO THE OK CORRAL, IN TOMBSTONE, ARIZONA TERRITORY.

Just ahead of him were Ike and Billy Clanton along with Tom and Frank McLaury on either side. Marching toward them were town Marshal Virgil Earp and his brothers, Morgan and Wyatt, along with Doc Holiday. Seconds later, gunshots echoed through the vacant lot at the end of Fremont Street. Claiborne squeezed off two shots at Virgil, missed. He and Ike Clanton broke into a run to the safety of C.S. Fly's photo studio. In the meantime, Billy Clanton and the two McLaurys lay dead. Morgan and Virgil Earp suffered wounds.

Ironically, Claiborne was recruited to help the Clantons and McLaurys even the odds in the expected confrontation that would become known as *Gunfight at the OK Corral.* Claiborne was supposedly associated with *The Cowboys,* a loose association of outlaw cattle rustlers and robbers in Pima and Cochise County, Arizona Territory. But, he tried downplaying his role in the *gunfight,* contending he wasn't armed at the time. Although he ended up testifying at the OK Corral inquest, his reputation suffered because he had fled the scene of the shootout. He disappeared for about a year.

Born in Yazoo County, Mississippi, Claiborne grew up working as a ranch hand, miner, and even helped John Slaughter drive cattle from Texas to the Tombstone area in 1880. Claiborne had a bit of an arrogant streak. When Pat Garrett killed William *Billy the Kid* Bonney in the summer of 1881, Claiborne decided he wanted to be known as Billy the Kid. Just why he earned such a right, as he called it, is unclear. He claimed to have killed three men who refused to honor his demand. But the only evidence of any gunfight involvement was in Charleston in Cochise County in October when he and James Hickey got into an argument over the issue. Hickey had been taunting him for using the name *Billy the Kid,* and Claiborne responded by drilling him between the eyes. He stood trial, but was acquitted.

Claiborne returned to Tombstone in November 1882 and, on the night of the 14th, got involved in an argument with gunman *Buckskin* Frank Leslie, a man with a reputation as a cold-blooded killer. Early that morning, Leslie refused to call Claiborne *Billy the Kid,* and the two men exchanged bitter words while drinking at the Oriental Saloon. According to the bartender, E. H. Dean, they got into a shoving match during an argument over politics. An angry Claiborne threatened Leslie, and stomped out.

"The next I hear was a man came running in telling Mr. Leslie that Claiborne was outside with a rifle to kill him," Dean said.

As Leslie left through a side door, he spotted Claiborne with a Winchester. "Billy, don't shoot," Leslie said. "I don't want you to kill me, nor do I want to have to shoot you."

Claiborne fired from about fifteen-feet away, but missed. Leslie drew his revolver and snapped off two shots. At least one hit Claiborne, who lived for only about half an hour after being shot. According to a statement by Leslie, Claiborne raised the rifle and shot first. A witnessed backed up the story. William Henry Bush, a local bootblack, told the *Tombstone Epitaph* that Claiborne said aloud, while walking toward the saloon, that he was going to kill Leslie. According to Bush, he warned Billy not to carry out his threat. But Claiborne even threatened him.

"No, you black son of a bitch, I will kill you," Claiborne told Bush. Seconds later, Bush said, "I saw him raise the gun to shoot Mr. Leslie, and I seen the gun go off, the bullet striking the sidewalk."

Authorities ruled the killing justified because Claiborne was waiting to ambush Leslie. Claiborne was 22.

FORTY-NINE

GUNMAN & POET

THE BANDIT STREAKED FROM THE HILLSIDE TAKING THE STAGE
DRIVER BY SURPRISE, FORCING THE COACH TO A STOP WITHOUT
A SHOT BEING FIRED.

A flour sack, with two holes cut out for the eyes, covered the
robber's head. He wore a long, soiled black duster over his clothes,
a 12-gauge shotgun braced against his shoulder.

"Throw down the strongbox, driver," the man ordered, and
then glanced to his right and his left. "If he dares shoot, give him
a solid volley boys."

The nervous and frightened driver looked right and left, as
well, and noticed what he determined were several rifles protrud-
ing from scattered boulders. After the robbery, the driver waited
until the bandit was out of sight, drove the stage a short distance,
and then jumped down and walked back to the scene of the robbery. The *rifles* he thought were trained on him, he discovered,
amounted to nothing more than sticks.

The stagecoach robbery was the work of Black Bart, who worked alone, but always tried to give the illusion others were waiting to back him up. The English-born outlaw operated mostly in and around southern California and southern Oregon during the 1870s and 1880s, establishing a reputation as one of the most notorious stagecoach robbers in the American West. *Chester Earl Bowles,* his real name, targeted Wells Fargo stages for most of his robberies, between 1875-1883. He's credited, or blamed, for nearly thirty holdups, and without firing a shot.

Dubbed a gentleman bandit, he sometimes left behind a poem in the Wells Fargo safe he had taken from the stagecoach. Black Bart, a man in his mid-fifties, also displayed a streak of chivalry during some robberies. During one robbery, a woman passenger threw her purse from the stagecoach window, but Black Bart picked it up and returned it.

"Madam," he said, "I do not wish your money."

Accounts of his robberies point out that Black Bart was always courteous, especially to women, and refused to take their jewelry or money. Despite so many robberies, Black Bart netted only about $18,000 from Wells Fargo. The company's private police force spent several years hunting for the bandit. When he was arrested, he was using the name Charles E. Bolton, a name he had been using for years while living in San Francisco. Bowles was tried, convicted, and sent to San Quentin prison where he served four years, and received a pardon.

Released January 1888, Bowles returned to his room at Nevada House, visibly aged, with failing eyesight, and hard of hearing. One of the reporters, on hand to greet him, asked if he intended to hold up any more stagecoaches.

"No, gentleman, I'm through with crime."

Asked if he would continue to write poetry, Bowles laughed.

"Now didn't you hear me say that I am through with crime?"

One month later, Black Bart disappeared. Wells Fargo managed to track him to the Palace Hotel in Visalia, but detectives never found him. Waiting in the room was his valise, which contained a can on corned beef, a can of tongue, a pound of coffee, and other assorted food items.

He was never heard from again.

FIFTY

MASTER
OF THE CON

"SUCKERS HAVE NO BUSINESS WITH MONEY, ANYHOW," SAID A MAN BY THE NAME OF CANADA BILL JONES, ONE OF HISTORY'S GREATEST CARD SHARPS.

Jones, born in Yorkshire, England, in the early 1800s, immigrated to Canada when he was about twenty. In Canada, he mastered three-card Monte, which is not a game, but a scam or swindle. After several years of fleecing suckers in Canada, he traveled into the US and took his game to the pre-war south where he conned passengers on Mississippi riverboats out of enormous sums of money.

Much of Jones success was attributed to playing the rube. He spoke in a squeaky voice, draped baggy clothes over his 130-pound frame, and came across as a bumbling greenhorn, a klutz that few people took seriously. But, that's where they made their mistake.

Jones was anything but klutzy. He was a master of the con and a renowned poker cheat. After the Civil War, he and his cardsharp partner, George Devol, decided to ply their trade on the railroad, targeting passengers who were heading west at the beginning of the country's ambitious expansion.

They were so successful that Canada Bill wrote the general superintendent of the Union Pacific Railroad offering $25,000 a year for the exclusive right to operate a three-card Monte on the trains. Bill promised to fleece only "the wealthy, and Methodist ministers." Not surprisingly, the railroad declined to accept the offer. When he became too well known on the railroad circuit, he traveled to racetracks throughout the country.

Canada Bill's weakness was his strength: Gambling. He enjoyed playing cards, even against other cheats. Once, his friend Devol warned him a Faro game he'd been playing was rigged. "Sure," said Bill, "but it was the only game in town." Among his most ardent admirers were other gamblers.

When Canada Bill died in 1880 in Reading, Pennsylvania, he was penniless. Dozens of gamblers showed up at his funeral, and raised money to repay the city for the cost of burying Bill, and to erect a gravestone in his honor.

One cardsharp, at the funeral, bet $100 that "Bill is not in that box."

FIFTY-ONE

THE HANGING
OF MARY SURRATT

A T 1:26 P.M., ON A WARM AND SUNNY JULY 7, 1865, A SPECIAL SIGNAL ALERTED TWO SOLDIERS STANDING BENEATH A GALLOWS TO KNOCK AWAY THE SUPPORTING BEAMS WITH LONG POLES.

Within seconds, four trapdoors snapped downward and four bodies dropped a few feet through the openings before the ropes around their necks jerked them back up with a savage swiftness. All four were hanged as convicted conspirators in the assassination of President Abraham Lincoln. Among the four: *Mary Surratt*, a 42-year old widow, the first woman ever hanged by the U.S. government.

The others were *Lewis Powell, David Herold, and George Atzerodt.* Surratt and the others were left dangling for about one-half hour before the bodies were cut down and placed atop crude gun boxes, which served as coffins. After doctors examined the bodies, they were buried in shallow graves next to the gallows in the prison yard of the Washington Arsenal Penitentiary.

A debate over Surratt's conviction and death sentence has waged for the last 148 years. Many believed Surratt would be spared the gallows because she was a woman. Surratt owned a boarding house where authorities believed John Wilkes Booth devised his plan to assassinate Lincoln. Five members of the military commission, which tried her case, sent a message to President Andrew Johnson recommending mercy, urging him to commute the death sentence to life imprisonment. Johnson, according to one source, claimed he never received such a request. Another report, however, quoted the president as saying he would not be willing to commute the sentence of the woman who "kept the nest that hatched the egg."

Two years after the hanging, the remains of the co-conspirators were removed from their graves and placed in a nearby storage building. In 1869, President Johnson allowed family members to claim the bodies. Three of the four were claimed, but not the one identified as Lewis Powell. The building where the four were tried and convicted remains standing today. It's called Grant Hall, located at Fort McNair in Washington.

FIFTY-TWO

A GOOD DAY TO DIE

THE 20-YEAR OLD STOOD ROCK SOLID STILL, ALMOST NONCHA-LANT, WHEN THE NOOSE SLIPPED OVER HIS HEAD AND AROUND HIS THROAT.

"Any last words?" he was asked.

"I came here to die, not to make a speech," said the young man.

The name *Crawford Goldsby*, didn't necessarily strike fear in the hearts of men—even when he killed for the first time at age 12. A few years later, he started calling himself Cherokee Bill, a name no one would soon forget. Hard to believe that Cherokee Bill, as a teen-ager, would become one of the most feared men in Indian Territory.

Born on Feb. 8, 1876, at Fort Concho, Texas, Goldsby moved with his mother to Fort Gibson in Indian Territory when he was seven. He then attended Indian school in Cherokee, Kansas, for three years, and spent another two in Indian school in Carlisle, Pennsylvania. Historians differ on the specifics of Goldsby's life after he returned home to Oklahoma. Cherokee Bill, according to one account, shot and killed his own brother-in-law who had told him to feed the hogs. He escaped prosecution because of his age.

In 1889, when his mother remarried, he turned rebellious and began a downward slide, drinking, and committing petty thefts. A couple of years later, he moved to the home of his sister, Georgia, and her husband. By age sixteen, he had learned to handle a gun and was considered a crack shot, and went to work for a ranch. At age 18, in the spring of 1894, he joined up with outlaws Jim and Bill Cook. Although the gang only rode together for less than a year, they waged a campaign of terror across Indian Territory.

A posse that carried a warrant for Jim Cook tracked down Cherokee Bill and the Cooks. In the gun battle that followed, Cherokee Bill shot and killed lawman Sequoyah Houston, managed to escape, and raced to the home of another sister, Maud Brown to hideout. When Cherokee Bill witnessed his sister's drunken husband, George Brown, beating up on her with a whip, he crept up behind the man and shot him to death.

A short time later, Cherokee Bill and Bill Cook recruited another gang. This one, made up of black men with Indian blood, began a crime spree across Oklahoma Territory stealing horses, robbing banks, retail stores, and stagecoaches, and shooting anyone who got in their way. Cherokee Bill was responsible for the death of seven men during his brief, but violent career. The law began closing in on him after he had killed an innocent passerby, Ernest Melton, while robbing a general store in Lenapah. Although he got away, Cherokee Bill was final captured on Dec. 31, 1894, when he robbed the train station at Nowat, Oklahoma.

Judge Isaac Parker, the Hanging Judge, conducted the trial, and characterized Cherokee Bill as a "bloodthirsty mad dog who kills for the love of killing." He also dubbed the outlaw as "the most vicious" of all the outlaws in the Oklahoma Territory. Although he was found guilty in federal court and sentenced to die, he filed an appeal with the Supreme Court. While awaiting word from the court, Cherokee Bill attempted to escape from the jail at Fort Smith. The escape was foiled but, in the process, he shot and killed guard Lawrence Keating.

Another trial was held. Another conviction handed down. Another death was declared. A few months later, in December 1895, the Supreme Court upheld the conviction in the first murder trial. As a result, Judge Parker scheduled the execution. On the day of his execution, March 17, 1896, Cherokee Bill and his police escort emerged from the courthouse.

The prisoner squinted into the sunlight, and said to no one in particular, "It is a good day to die." Minutes later, Crawford Goldsby—alias Cherokee Bill—was dangling from a rope. He was 20 years of age.

Even though he had already been executed, Crawford Goldsby's second appeal to the Supreme Court was still pending. In May 1896, the Department of Justice sent a letter to US Attorney James Read at Fort Smith, wanted to know if the judgment in the first case had been carried out.

FIFTY-THREE

ROSE OF
THE WILD BUNCH

MOST PARENTS CONSIDER THEMSELVES ROLE MODELS AND, FOR THE MOST PART, WARM TO THE IDEA OF THE KIDS FOLLOWING IN THEIR FOOTSTEPS, BUT NOT ALWAYS.

Laura Bullion was born near Knickerbocker, or Mertzon, Texas, in late 1876, although there's some uncertainty as to the exact place and date. Her mother was a German immigrant. Henry Bullion, her Native-American father, was an outlaw and, as it turns out, Laura's role model. The moment she became a teen-ager, Laura Bullion bought a one-way ticket to ride. When she was 13, her father introduced Laura to William Carver, also an outlaw. He had been married to Bullion's aunt Viana Byler, who died from a fever.

When Carver began his romantic relationship with 15-year old Laura, he was already involved with Josie Bassett, a female outlaw.

For the next couple of years, Laura worked as a prostitute at a brothel in San Antonio, one apparently frequented by the Wild Bunch outlaw gang, which was also used as a hideout. Carver joined the Wild Bunch when he was on the run from the law. Laura's relationship with Carver cooled and she took up with Ben Kilpatrick and helped him rob banks.

After one of the robberies, the two of them made their way to Robbers' Roost in Utah in 1898 to join up with the Wild Bunch, led by Butch Cassidy. Other members of the gang included Carver, Harry Longbaugh – known as the Sundance Kid – Harvey Logan, George Curry, Elzy Lay and Henry Wilber Meeks. In addition to taking part in several train robberies, Laura also helped fence the money and the goods stolen by the gang. She was known to the group as Della Rose, and sometimes referred to as "Rose of the Wild Bunch." After several big-money train and bank robberies, the end was in sight for the Wild Bunch.

- Aug. 29,1900: Robs Union Pacific train at Tipton, Wyoming, of $50,000

- Sept. 19,1900: Robs First National Bank, Winnemucca, Nevada, of $32,640

- April 1, 1901: Authorities ambush Carver and Kilpatrick at Sonora, Texas. Carver is shot and dies of his wounds while Kilpatrick escapes.

- July 3, 1901: Robs Great Northern Train, near Wagner, Montana, of $65,000

Less than four months later, authorities arrested Bullion and Kilpatrick in St. Louis. Kilpatrick, found guilty of robbery, was sentenced to 15 years in prison. She was charged with robbery and forgery of signatures to banknotes and got five years. The arrest report listed her profession as prostitute; it also noted that Bullion was masquerading as Mrs. Nellie Rose when she was apprehended.

Bullion apparently kept out of trouble and was released from the Missouri State Penitentiary on Sept. 19, 1905. When she left prison, Bullion headed to Memphis, Tennessee, where, under an assumed name, she went to work as a seamstress and dressmaker. She never again saw Kilpatrick. Jail time didn't cure him of his criminal ways. Soon after being released from prison in June 1911, he attempted to rob a Southern Pacific express near Sanderson, Texas, and was killed with an ice mallet.

Bullion gave up her criminal ways and established herself as an interior decorator. She suffered some financial hardships in the Fifties, and died Dec. 2, 1961, of heart disease. Her grave marker at Memorial Park Cemetery in Memphis reads:

Freda Bullion Lincoln

Laura Bullion

The Thorny Rose

1876 - 1961

The headstone is decorated with a rose and embossed rose vines along the border. "The Thorny Rose" referred to Bullion's other nickname given her by the Wild Bunch.

FIFTY-FOUR

THE UNREAL
MCCOY

BILL McCOY SAT ALONE IN CLEVELAND BROTHERS' SALOON IN LUSK, WYOMING, ON A COLD JANUARY NIGHT IN 1887, DRINKING IN EXCESS. HE HEARD WHISPERS AND FELT STARES, ALL BECAUSE OF A RECENT SERIES OF NEWSPAPER ARTICLES IN THE LUSK *HERALD*.

In the articles, editor J.K. Calkins suggested McCoy was actually *Dan Bogan,* a man wanted for two murders in Texas. Author Robert K. DeArment; in his book *Deadly Dozen*, described Bogan as one of the most underrated gunman of the 19th century American frontier. Bogan, born in Alabama in 1860, grew up in Texas. He started working as a cowboy early in life and, before long, carved a reputation as a man with a quick temper and an always-ready-to-fight attitude. After a wage dispute, he was blacklisted in Texas and left the state for Wyoming, settling in *Lusk*, situated in the eastern part of the state, about twenty miles from Nebraska.

Despite an angry, howling high plains wind, a few thirsty cowboys ducked inside the Cleveland Brothers' saloon in Lusk. They noticed the drunker McCoy got, the angrier he became, telling anyone who would listen that Calkins better find another subject to write about. Concerned about McCoy's strident behavior, the bartender summoned town constable Charlie Gunn. The former Texas Ranger managed to calm down McCoy and convinced him to call it a night.

McCoy would have been smart to use the opportunity to pull up stakes and leave Lusk. But he didn't. A few days, later, he renewed his bellyaching, but this time at Jim Walters' saloon. Gunn showed up again and this time issued a stern warning. Although he left, McCoy returned to the same saloon the next morning, January 15th. When he arrived, he saw Gunn sitting at a table. As the 32-year old lawman rose to meet him, McCoy yanked a gun from his holster and fired, dropping Gunn to the floor with a bullet in his gut.

McCoy walked up the lawman, placed the gun at the wounded man's head, and squeezed off another round. Gunn raced out of the saloon, climbed into the saddle of the first horse he saw, and bolted down the street. Deputy Johnny Owens, armed with a shotgun, stepped into the street, fired a warning round, but McCoy didn't turn around. Owens fired again. The buckshot slammed into McCoy's shoulder, knocking him out of the saddle into the street.

Despite the wound, he escaped from jail that night, but later turned himself in because the shoulder wound worsened. Owens eventually escorted Bogan, alias *Bill McCoy*, to Cheyenne for trial. The case dragged on for months. In September 1887, Bogan was convicted guilty of first-degree murder, and sentenced to hang. Less than a month later, Bogan and three others sawed through the quarter-inch iron ceiling of their cell and escaped. Authorities posted a thousand-dollar reward for Bogan's capture, dead or alive. It's believed that Bogan may have traveled to New Orleans and sailed to Argentina. Pinkerton detective *Charlie Siringo,* however, felt certain that Bogan returned and assumed yet another alias.

In 1903, the *Lusk Herald* reported that McCoy fell from a horse in New Mexico and died from a broken neck. A letter was found in his pocket revealing his true identity. "Many persons here will be glad to learn of his demise as the crime he committed in this town was a cold-blooded one."

Nevertheless, Dan Bogan cheated justice and got away with murder.

FIFTY-FIVE

GUNPLAY AT THE LONG BRANCH

BUFFALO HUNTER LEVI RICHARDSON WALKED INTO THE LONG BRANCH SALOON IN DODGE CITY ON A COLD, WINDY SPRING EVENING IN 1879, ORDERED A DRINK, AND SAT DOWN NEAR A POT-BELLIED STOVE WHERE HE HAD A CLEAR VIEW OF THE FRONT ENTRANCE.

Richardson watched and waited, determined to confront his former friend, professional gambler Frank Loving. Bad blood flowed between the two over differences stemming from Richardson's affection for Loving's wife, Mattie. After waiting late into the evening, Richardson hadn't seen any sign of Loving so he decided to leave. Just as he started for the front door, Loving walked in.

The Dodge City, Kansas, saloon experienced its share of gunplay over the years, and this night would be no exception. Richardson motioned him over to a long table where they sat down and eventually got involved in a bitter exchange of words. A short time later, the two men stood up, eyeball-to-eyeball, belly-to-belly, glaring at each other, with hands on the handles of their six-shooters. According to witnesses, Richardson drew first, prompting the 19-year old Loving to go for his own pistol. Both men began shooting at each other. Gunsmoke filled the Long Branch, and customers scattered to avoid the spray of bullets.

Several doors to the east of the Long Branch, Dodge City Marshal Charlie Bassett heard the shooting and quickly made his way to the saloon. With the help of Deputy Sheriff Duffey, Bassett separated and disarmed the two men. Bassett found Loving's Remington No. 44 empty; Richardson had emptied his gun of five shots. Duffey threw Richardson into a chair. But the wounded man struggled to his feet, staggered toward the billiard table, and fell to the floor. The buffalo hunter lay dead from wounds to his chest and side. He was 28.

Loving, miraculously, escaped injury except for a slight scratch on the hand. Two days later, a coroner's inquest ruled that Loving shot Richardson in self-defense, and he was released. He would later leave his wife and two children, and move to Las Vegas, New Mexico, also known for its lawlessness. Loving would leave Las Vegas in 1882 and make his way to Trinidad, Colorado, where another confrontation awaited, as you'll read in the next story.

FIFTY-SIX

THE TRINIDAD GUNFIGHT

A GLARING SUN FILLED MAIN STREET IN TRINIDAD, COLORADO, ON APRIL 15, 1882, AS TWO PROFESSIONAL GAMBLERS STOOD FACING EACH OTHER TO SETTLE A BITTER DISPUTE OVER GAM-BLING DEBTS.

Frank Loving worked as a Faro dealer at the Bank Exchange Saloon. John Allen worked at the Imperial Saloon. The two knew each other from their days in Dodge City. The anger between the two men had been brewing for months, mostly over cards games and house loans. As they started walking toward each other, cooler heads prevailed and stopped the showdown. But the argument was far from over. Loving, three years earlier, had killed Levi Richardson at Dodge City's Long Branch Saloon in a gunfight over Richardson's affections toward the gambler's wife.

Trinidad, at the time, was a prosperous community, thanks to the discovery of coal in 1872. It drew a diverse cultural mix of families, many of them Europeans with mining experience. The growing community attracted several now-legendary characters, including Wyatt Earp, Doc Holliday, Billy the Kid, and Clay Allison. Bat Masterson and his brother, Jim, served as town marshals for a time.

The enforced truce between Loving and Allen didn't last long. On the following evening, a Sunday, "Cockeyed" Frank, as he was called, walked into the Imperial Saloon. When Allen spotted him, he pulled his gun and fired. The pair exchanged gunfire but failed to hit each other. Allen decided to leave the saloon by a rear door. Deputy Marshal Jim Masterson heard the shooting and hurried to the Imperial and confiscated Loving's pistol. He went searching for Allen, but couldn't find him. When Masterson returned to the Imperial, he discovered Loving got hold of two other guns. Again, Masterson disarmed Loving. After lawman left to find Allen, Loving slipped out the door and entered George Hammond's hardware store for another gun and ammo. But he had no idea that Allen had followed him.

At the sound of gunfire, Masterson arrived at the hardware store to see Loving stumble out, mumbling, "Jim, I'm shot," a bullet in the back. Marshal Lou Kreeger found Allen hiding at the rear of the store, placed him under arrest and carted him off to jail. Five days later, on April 21st, Loving died because the bullet couldn't be removed. He was 28.

Allen went on trial for murder in September 1882, but was found not guilty and returned to Dodge City. Sometime later, he became a preacher and traveling evangelist.

FIFTY-SEVEN

BORDER QUEEN BETRAYED

TRIGGER-HAPPY AND QUICK-TEMPERED COWBOYS TURNED CALDWELL, KANSAS, INTO ONE OF THE MORE VIOLENT TOWNS ALONG THE AMERICAN FRONTIER.

Known as the *Border Queen*, Caldwell served as destination for nearly 100,000 head of Texas longhorns between 1882 and 1883. Months of driving longhorn cattle along dry, dusty and wind-swept ranges and trails, left drovers restless, and eager to unwind. And, did a lot of it in Caldwell. Behavior in Caldwell was rowdy. A lot of people died. At the same time, saloons and gambling establishments registered high profits. Law was almost non-existent. In fact, a Caldwell lawman didn't last long—until Henry Newton Brown rode into town. But, Brown harbored a dark secret.

When he arrived in Caldwell, Brown had been on the run from two murder warrants in New Mexico in connection with the

Lincoln County war. He was twenty-five when he drifted into the rugged Kansas cow town in July 1882. With him was William Sherod Brown, alias *Ben Wheeler*. Brown landed a job as assistant town marshal. Five months later, he was named marshal. He named Wheeler as deputy marshal. Caldwell's long history of violence earned it a reputation as tough as Dodge City and Abilene. But Brown and Wheeler managed to bring things under control.

The local newspaper described Brown as "one of the quickest men on the trigger in the Southwest." He also married, bought a home, and settled down. Residents described him as *undersize*— a man who didn't "smoke, drink, chew, or gamble." At the same time, the citizens of Caldwell admired him so much that they honored him with an engraved silver- and gold-mounted Winchester rifle.

Brown's dark past, however, began to emerge. The marshal had once ridden with Billy the Kid. Both were involved in New Mexico's Lincoln County War between ranchers, merchants, and corrupt politicians. Brown, and the Kid, ambushed and killed the sheriff there. A few days later, Brown shot someone else to death. As the chief law officer of Caldwell, however, he managed to buy himself some breathing room. At the same time, though, he began worrying about family financial issues, searching for other ways to fatten his paycheck. Along with Wheeler, the marshal approached city officials and got their blessing to track a killer into Indian Territory. Brown had a plan in mind, but it had nothing to do will tracking anyone.

Once away from Caldwell, he formed a small gang that included Wheeler, and two other friends, William Smith and John Wesley. All four set their sights on the bank in Medicine Lodge, Kansas. Things went downhill fast during the robbery. Brown gunned down the bank president and Wheeler killed one of the clerks. The small gang fled, but was captured a short time later by a local posse.

Although the four of them were behind bars, the jail couldn't keep out an angry lynch mob. Brown and Wheeler tried to get away. One member of the mob took aim and filled Brown with a load of buckshot, killing him. Wheeler, suffering from a gunshot wound, was dragged along with the other two members to an elm tree and hanged. Ironically, the rifle Brown used to kill the bank president was the same one Winchester presented to him by the citizens of Caldwell for his success in bringing law and order to the town.

FIFTY-EIGHT

IMMORTALIZED
IN A PAINTING

ON THE AFTERNOON OF MARCH 20, 1868, SEVERAL MEN— BELIEVED TO BE MEMBERS OF THE JAMES-YOUNGER GANG—WALKED INTO THE NIMROD LONG BANKING CO. IN RUSSELLVILLE, KENTUCKY. TWO OTHERS REMAINED OUTSIDE.

One of the men approached bank President Nimrod Long and asked him to change a $50 bill. Long, however, refused, suggesting the bill was counterfeit. Seconds later, Long found himself staring down the barrel of a six-gun that he said later belonged to either Jesse James or Cole Younger. Long struggled with the gunman, and then decided to make a run for it. Before he got to the back door, a shot echoed through the bank and a bullet creased the banker's scalp, sending him to the floor.

Playing possum, he managed to shake off the effects of the wound, got up, and made his way outside. After forcing the employees, at gunpoint, to fill wheat sacks with money, the four inside joined the pair waiting outside the bank and raced out of Russellville, firing their guns into the air. The gang escaped with $9,035.92. And, according to one account, the gang didn't know there was an additional $50,000 in the vault. The bank, situated on the city square, remains the same as it was in 1868, but now restored as an apartment building. It displays a large mural depicting the hold-up. The city of Russellville conducts a re-enactment of the robbery during the annual Tobacco and Heritage Festival.

The James gang had made history by staging the country's first daylight bank robbery about three years earlier. Despite the eyewitness accounts in Russellville, Jesse James denied having anything to do with the robbery, saying that he had been visiting relatives at Chaplin, Kentucky, near Bardstown on that day. Brother Frank denied taking part, as well. Cole Younger, a few years later, said he couldn't have been involved because he was herding cattle in Ellis County, Texas.

One of the gang members, George Sheperd, was convicted of the robbery and sent to prison for three years. His cousin, Oliver Sheperd, was gunned down attempting to avoid arrest. The James Gang, following the Russellville robbery, thundered its way through history by robbing and pillaging additional banks, and other places and people.

FIFTY-NINE

A LIFE OF ALIBIS & EXCUSES

THOMAS COLEMAN "COLE" YOUNGER WAS BORN IN 1844 NEAR LEES SUMMIT, MISSOURI, THE SON OF A PROMINENT FARMER AND ONE OF 14 CHILDREN.

Members of the Kansas Militia killed his father and the tragedy no doubt framed Cole's thinking that he lived in an unjust society. As a teen-ager, Cole and his brother, James—along with Frank and Jesse James—rode with William Clarke Quantrill's Confederate raiders during the Civil War. All were involved in the infamous *Lawrence Kansas Massacre* in which over 150 men were killed. The slaughter was so cold-blooded and heinous that even the Confederate government abhorred its violence. Quantrill's guerrillas reined havoc where they rode.

After the war, the Youngers—Cole, Jim, John, and Bob—joined forced with the James' brothers and initiated a spree of robberies that included banks, trains, and stagecoaches, along with committing a string of other crimes. In Early February 1866, the gang staged the first peacetime daylight bank robbery in the US. Two year later, it struck a bank in Russellville, Kentucky. Despite attempts to romanticize them and others of the same era, these men led lives of crime and violence. At least eleven citizens were killed during the robberies.

The glory days of the James-Younger Gang ended on Sept. 8, 1876, in a hail of bullets in Northfield, Minnesota, during a robbery attempt at the First National Bank. The gang attempted a bold, daytime bank robbery, but things went bad fast. Frank and Jesse James managed to escape. But, Cole and his brothers, Jim and Bob, were badly wounded. To avoid being hanged, the Youngers admitted guilt and were sentenced to life in prison at the Minnesota State Prison at Stillwell.

When asked about the robbery, Cole admitted, "We tried a desperate game and lost. But we are rough men used to rough ways, and we will abide by the consequences." While serving time, Cole founded the *Prison Mirror*, a newspaper aimed at shedding "a ray of light upon the lives of those behind the bars." The inmate publication still operates to this day.

Bob Younger died in prison on September 16, 1889, of tuberculosis. Cole and Jim were paroled on July 10, 1901. Jim committed suicide in a hotel room in St Paul, Minnesota, on October 19, 1902. Cole succeeded in obtaining a pardon in 1903. He eventually hooked up with Frank James and lectured on "What My Life Has Taught Me." They also operated a Wild West show.

Cole Younger rarely owned up to any crime he committed, and always denied being involved—except for the one that sent him to prison. In reality, however, criminals lie and deny all the time. In his autobiography, Younger portrayed himself as a Confederate *avenger* more than an outlaw. In fact, he owned up to only *one* crime: the Northfield Raid in which he was caught. If he hadn't been caught, there's no doubt he would have denied involvement. His book, by the way, is available now as a free Kindle download, *The Story of Cole Younger, by Himself.* The original title read as follows:

The Story of Cole Younger by Himself: Being an autobiography of the Missouri Guerrilla Captain and Outlaw, His Capture and Prison Life, And the Only Authentic Account of the Northfield Raid Ever Published.

Cole Younger died on March 21, 1916.

SIXTY

OUTLAWS WHO RODE THE RAILS

AMERICA'S EXPANSION TO THE PACIFIC OCEAN WAS DESCRIBED BY THEODORE ROOSEVELT AS, "THE GREAT LEAP WESTWARD."

Completion of the Transcontinental Railroad served as the lynchpin in America's expansion strategy. By the time the War Between the States ended in 1865, more than 30,000 miles of railroad track stretched from coast-to-coast. Two major events triggered this era of dramatic growth: (1) Passage of the Homestead Act in 1862, which provided 160-acre lots free to anyone who agreed to live on the land for five years and make improvements to it. (2) California Gold Rush, which lured people west in record numbers, forcing the state to expand agriculture and ranching as mining boomtowns sprung up along the tracks to accommodate basic needs of settlers.

As the system expanded across the country, so did crime against railroads. No organized police units were in place when railroads were first built. Law enforcement, for the most part, was left to vigilante groups, but they weren't very effective. The end of the war complicated the situation because a significant number of unemployed soldiers scattered to rail yards and rail cars, where they survived by robbing, looting, and generally becoming a growing danger to society.

In order to combat the alarming upswing in theft and robbery, and the lack of effective law enforcement, railroads began implementing their own police forces, hiring contractors to investigate millions of dollars in the loss of freight and luggage. Crime spiraled even higher when outlaws began boarding trains, robbing passengers, and stealing from freight and express cars.

The first known train robbery took place at the end of the Civil War, May 5, 1865, when an Ohio & Mississippi express train was derailed just outside Cincinnati. The crime was never solved. About a year and a half later, masked men boarded another O&M train in Seymour, Indiana, and relieved it of $45,000. The railroad hired Allan Pinkerton to investigate, and he identified the robbers as the Reno Brothers Gang. From that point, well-organized outlaw gangs grew more daring, dynamiting bridges and tracks, blowing up rail cars and, in some cases, even railroad stations. Among the more infamous were:

- Hole in the Wall Gang, led by Robert Leroy Parker (Butch Cassidy) and Harry Longbaugh (The Sundance Kid).

- Wild Bunch.

- James Gang.

- Younger Brothers.

Years later, four brothers formed the infamous Dalton Gang that specialized in making life miserable for rail passengers and freight haulers. Ironically, several years before the gang was formed, a highly respected Deputy U.S. Marshal by the name of Frank Dalton was shot and killed while making an arrest in November 1887. During these train robberies, passengers and crewmembers were wounded or killed, which increased the demand for railroads to maintain their own police forces.

Eastern railroads used the term detective for their officers. Their counterparts in the West were called police officers or special agents. Pinkerton and Bat Masterson were among the most famous special agents. Desperate to stem mounting crime, railroads often hired individuals regardless of experience or background. The general criteria favored men who were big, strong, aggressive, and could handle a gun. The combined efforts of railroad detectives, Texas Rangers, and US. Marshals were effective as the 19th century drew to a close, and set the stage for the demise of train robbery escapades.

SIXTY-ONE

DEACON
OF DEATH

A LONG-RUNNING FEUD BETWEEN SHERIFF BUD FRAZER AND *DEACON JIM* MILLER CAME TO A BOILING POINT WHEN THEY CONFRONTED EACH OTHER ON A PECOS, TEXAS, STREET ON APRIL 12, 1894.

Frazer, four year earlier, had been elected county sheriff. A year later, he hired J.B Miller as deputy—a decision he would come to regret. Most of the people in Pecos liked Miller. He wore a badge, went to church with regular frequency with his wife and child, and even read aloud from the Bible. But, things were not as they seemed. Hiding behind Miller's polite demeanor was a stone-cold killer with a sinister stare and hair-trigger temper.

Deadly *Deacon Jim* Miller, as he would later be called, was born in Arkansas in 1866, orphaned early, and sent to live with his grand-parents in Texas. It didn't take long before Miller began building his reputation as a gunman. In fact, he once claimed that when he was eight, he killed his grandparents, but authorities declined to consider an eight-year old the main suspect in a double-murder. It's believed that Miller copped to the killings as a way of creating an aura about himself as an adult. As a teen-ager, however, his taste for killing emerged for real. Miller went to live with his uncle, but murdered him. This time, the law took him seriously, arrested him, and eventually sentenced him to life in prison. A legal technicality, however, won him his freedom.

Miller decided to become a killer-for-hire and even advertised his skills, charging $150 per kill. In the early 1880s, when he was living in San Saba County, Texas, Miller's campaign to hire out as an assassin was paying off. Miller liked to kill from ambush, and didn't have a problem plugging someone in the back. A shotgun served as his weapon of choice. His list of victims included lawmen, cattle ranchers, and political figures. He was also implicated in the death of famed Sheriff Pat Garrett, who killed Billy the Kid. Miller's actual body count remains a mystery. Various accounts put the number at eight. *Killer Jim,* as he was also known, claimed about 50. But anyone willing to shoot someone in the back from behind cover is likely to exaggerate now and again.

Deacon Jim always wore a long black coat, no matter what the weather, and Sheriff Frazer soon learned why. Knowing Miller's reputation with a shotgun, Frazier had no intention of giving Miller a fighting chance when they met. The two men felt only disdain as they faced each other just outside the hotel that Miller owned. With only a few feet separating them, the sheriff drew his .44 and squeezed off four shots. At least three hit Miller in the chest. Another pierced his right arm. When Deacon Jim went down, Frazer knew the man was dead, so he turned and walked away. Hours later, Frazer express shock when he learned Miller was only slightly wounded.

Under the long frock coat, Deacon Jim wore a metal plate that absorbed the shock and killing power of the bullets—possibly the first known use in the Wild West of what would later be called a bulletproof vest. Frazier left Pecos to put distance between him and Miller. But Killer Miller was not the kind to forget a man who tried to kill him. A couple of years later, he tracked Frazer to Toyah, Texas, where the former lawman was working as a stable hand. Miller shoved a shotgun into Frazer's face and killed him.

The last time Miller used a shotgun was in the brutal slaying of retired US Marshall Gus Bobbitt. Three men (Jesse West, Berry Burrell and Joseph Allen) paid Miller $1,700 to assassinate the marshal. But Bobbit lived long enough to finger his killer. All four were taken into custody and put behind bars in Ada, Oklahoma. Up to this point, law enforcement experienced little success in convicting Miller for his crimes. Expert legal counsel, usually paid for by his wealthy clients, had always represented him. A mob, however, vowed to prevent any legal maneuvering from blocking the demands of justice.

Rather than chance a court appearance, the mob attacked the jail, broke into it, and dragged Miller and the three other outlaws to a nearby barn where they lynched them. Just before being hanged, Miller is reported to have shouted "Let 'er rip!" What a guy. Dead at 48.

SIXTY-TWO

THE DAY THEY HANGED
TOM HORN

"READY, TOM." WITH THOSE WORDS DEPUTY SHERIFF RICHARD PROCTOR OF CHEYENNE LOOPED A HANGMAN'S NOOSE AROUND THE NECK OF ONE-TIME LAWMAN-TURNED-OUTLAW TOM HORN.

Less than a minute later, on the morning of November 20, 1903, the trap door beneath the prisoner's feet snapped open and Horn dropped to his death. The once intimidating Horn, who stood six-feet and weighed about two-hundred pounds, won admiration from some of those attending the hanging for being the most composed man on the gallows platform that Friday morning.

Horn's journey to the gallows began on November 21, 1860, with his birth in Memphis, Missouri. He left home at 14 to escape the temper of an abusive father. Two years later, he became a

201

Cavalry scout and rose to become chief of scouts in the Southwest region and helped track down the notorious Geronimo.

Horn traveled to central Arizona where he got involved in the Pleasant Valley War of 1887. The *conflict*, which ignited over water and grazing rights, and disputes involving property borders, pitted cattlemen and sheep men against each other. Several men from each side lost their lives, but no one was able to name the killer or killers. Suspicions arose that Horn participated as a killer-for-hire, but no one could say which side bankrolled him.

In his autobiography, Horn contends he served as a deputy sheriff then, and helped mediate the conflict. Pinkerton Detective Agency became interested in Horn for his tracking abilities and hired him in 1890 to handle criminal cases mostly around Colorado and Wyoming. Pinkerton, however, parted ways with him four years later because of several accusations leveled against Horn.

Historical accounts of Horn's movements during this period reflect contradiction. According to one account, Horn worked as a US marshal and a range detective for several wealthy ranchers in Wyoming and Colorado at the same time he worked for Pinkerton. The report, however, claims Horn served as a hired gun for the Wyoming Cattle Grower's Association, and assembled a private army to attack homesteaders in the bloody Johnson County War.

No evidence was ever found showing that he participated in the fighting. Several years later, Horn joined the cavalry and fought in the Spanish-American War, and then returned to Wyoming to hunt rustlers once again.

On the morning of July 18, 1901, Horn carried out his last ambush when he hid in the brush along the Powder River Road, near Cheyenne, waiting for rancher Kels P. Nickell, a man he had seen only once. Nickell's 14-year old son, Willie—who was wearing his father's coat and hat—climbed aboard the wagon to guide it off the ranch property. When the kid jumped down to open the gate,

Horn fired from hiding. The bullet from his .30-30 rifle struck the boy. As the young man staggered to his feet to climb back into the wagon, Horn reportedly fired again. Willie Nickell slammed to the ground, dead.

Based on a questionable confession delivered after too much to drink, Horn got blamed for the killing. But there was no *direct* evidence against him. Ironically, a group of forensic experts exonerated Horn in 1993. During a re-staging of the trial, information surfaced that there might have been a second shooter involved in Willie Nickell's death.

During his last days among the living, Horn spent some of the time on a hobby—braiding horsehair and leather-works. One of the last photographs taken show him in a chair waving what would erroneously be referred to as the rope that would hang him.

His execution took place one day before his 43rd birthday. When Horn died, so did the era of gunfighters, road agents, and rustlers.

ABOUT THE AUTHOR

Tom Rizzo is a storyteller, blogger, and speaker. He writes novels, short stories, and nonfiction. His post-Civil War action-adventure novel, *Last Stand At Bitter Creek* ranked among the finalists for the 2013 Western Fictioneers' *Peacemaker Award* for Best First Novel.

A former journalist, Tom worked as a news broadcaster, spent several years with the Associated Press, and worked as a free-lance writer creating everything from magazine articles to advertising and promotional material for a broad range of businesses. During his writing journey, he met a colorful cast of characters who inspired him to consider telling stories of his own.

Tom grew up in Central Ohio, lived in Great Britain for several years, and now calls Houston, Texas, home. He is a member of *Western Writers of America, Wild West History Association,* and *Western Fictioneers.*

Learn more about Tom at *www.TomRizzo.com* where he writes blogs about Frontier America. He also interviews veteran and emerging storytellers from various genres. Connect with him:

- Email: *tom@tomrizzo.com*
- Facebook: *https://www.facebook.com/thomas.rizzo.writes*
- Twitter: *https://twitter.com/TomRizzoWrites*
- Amazon: *http://bit.ly/RizzoAmazon*

www.ingramcontent.com/pod-product-compliance
Lightning Source LLC
Chambersburg PA
CBHW060238050426
42448CB00009B/1492